The Battle for Home

MARWA AL-SABOUNI

The Battle for Home

The Vision of a Young Architect in Syria

Foreword by Roger Scruton

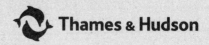

Contents

Foreword by **Roger Scruton**

It was no small surprise for me to receive, two years ago, an e-mail from Homs in Syria, asking me to explain something in my book *The Aesthetics of Architecture.* How could that book have reached Homs, of which I knew only because the tragedy of the Levant had occupied me over the last twenty years? And who was this person so eccentric as to devote time to issues of architectural aesthetics, when all around her the fabric of her ancient city was falling in ruins? I replied immediately, and very soon was in regular correspondence with one of the most remarkable people I have never met. Now she has written her own book, and it is the work of a profound thinker with a unique ability to address one of the most pressing questions confronting the people of the Middle East, which is the question of their built environment.

So far only two models have been proposed for a Middle Eastern city that is to be in communication with the modern world. One is Le Corbusier's plan for Algiers, which involves demolishing everything and trapping the traumatized populace in concrete blocks under motorways. The other is Dubai, a bombastic and profligate fun park of petrol-dollar materialism designed on computers in London for the global rich. The idea of a city in which prosperous and poor, old and young, Muslim and Christian, live peacefully side by side in streets that they share, beneath a skyline respectful of their religious aspirations – the idea represented by cities such as Homs, Aleppo and Damascus in the great moments of their past – has had no part to play in the plans of the futurist bureaucrats and modernist computer nerds. Yet, as Marwa al-Sabouni clearly shows, the plans imposed on cities like Homs by those charged with their public aspect have been major contributors to the conflicts that have now destroyed them.

The metropolis came into being in the Eastern Mediterranean, and has been the ancient solution to human difference – the way in which diverse communities settle side by side and imprint their agreements on the earth. Marwa al-Sabouni argues that the Syrian people must rediscover the feeling for place and materials, for the street, the façade and the shared skyline, that created their cities, which have endured in continuous occupation since ancient times. She gives a moving account of traditional Islamic architecture and the way in which its principles have been misunderstood or bowdlerized into architectural clichés. And she boldly criticizes the corruption that has surrendered her city to both materialist vandalism and hate-filled revenge. In all this she eloquently describes a Syrian city as it now is, in the midst of a conflict that we in Europe have so imperfectly understood, and the costs of which we shall have to bear.

This book is the moving record of one person's effort to stay loyal to her homeland, at a time of great suffering and personal distress. It tells a painful and tragic story. But it is also the expression of a beautiful soul, who comes to us out of a confused and dreadful battle with a message of hope.

Malmesbury, September 2015

Preface to the new edition by **Marwa al-Sabouni**

It has been over a year since the first edition of this book was published, during which time the war in my country has repeatedly failed to end. On the contrary, the conflict in cities such as Aleppo has escalated, causing more casualties and destroying more and more areas. In this book, I speak little about Aleppo and focus more on my home city of Homs, but the two cities have more than a newspaper headline to share. The story of Homs is the story of all Syrian cities: periods of prosperity and peace, followed by years of decline and eventual conflict. Today Aleppo stands in rubble, just as Homs does; torn apart, and bleeding. Both once had a treasured heart, which has been destroyed by this raging war, and both have shed blood, people and wreckage from those desperate districts that have been obliterated.

Is it a coincidence that the same dynamics have been repeated in the same kinds of places? That the most heated districts are those of mass housing, which all have one thing in common – soul-destroying, monotonous, isolated boxes thrown up on the outskirts, away from any city-related activity? Is it really far-fetched to relate this kind of built environment to conflict? My book argues that it cannot be more pertinent. It is not claiming that bad architecture and failing urbanism are solely responsible for a war that has resulted in regional destruction and global disruption: that is not the point. But it would be foolish to blind ourselves to the most evident contributor to our formation as inhabitants and, if we are lucky, citizens. Because we are what we build. Indeed, our built environment dictates more than we would like to admit; not only does it impact on our economic, social and cultural lives, but it also

– and more importantly – holds the values we trust in its elements; in every detail, our environment carries the seeds we plant in buildings when we erect them.

I wrote this book following my studies and observations of what was going on around me. However, after it was first published it became a window through which I made new connections with the world, and that has been a great gift to my heart. My mind has also been grateful, most of all to learn about the work of Jane Jacobs and Christopher Alexander, who have both touched brilliantly upon the importance of architecture and urbanism in keeping our cities, settlements and neighbourhoods *alive*. It is most assuredly a matter of life and death – at least this is what the Syrian war has proved to us.

This book tries to show how deleterious the ways of building in Syria have been, but also how they could be in the future. This is especially urgent now that the hammer of destruction is ongoing on the one hand, but on the other hand plans for reconstruction are already under examination in many places around the world. Even here in Syria, in places where conflict has passed, talks about reconstruction have taken the place of discussions about war, even among ordinary people. But this carries no real hope if we are going to repeat the same mistakes again – the mistakes that this book sheds light on through its narratives. It tries to show that this war could not be a more serious wake-up call for all of us to reflect on the importance of the role architecture plays in our destinies. It aims to show that, if we wish to avoid walking through the hells of such a war again, we must rebuild in a different way.

Homs, December 2016

Introduction

We in Syria have been in the news since 2011. The world has been watching us, and we have been watching ourselves, getting killed, tortured and uprooted. We have seen our buildings demolished, our cities destroyed and our archaeological treasures vandalized. These images have been on display so much that we rarely question why all this has happened. In politics and history, when narratives are assembled, parties tell their own sides of the story. It is only through architecture that we see the point of view that is no one's in particular and everyone's in general. Buildings do not lie to us: they tell the truth without taking sides. Every little detail in an urban configuration is an honest register of a lived story.

In this book, I try to show that in the built environment we can find not only indicators of events that have already occurred, but also portents of what *could* or *might* still occur. In addition, I try to show how architecture in my country has played a vital role in creating, directing and heightening conflicts between warring factions, by facilitating poor choices and narrowing viable alternatives. I write about the shape of settlements and related economic systems, the moral code inspired by the architecture of a place, and the ways in which architectural choices can determine questions of identity and home. Relating to another reason why I wrote this book, it should be noted that even in countries that seem to be distanced from our own misfortune in Syria (especially the other countries touched by the so-called Arab Spring), notions of identity and home are just as much in jeopardy.

The world has watched with anguish as ISIS has vandalized or threatened treasured sites, including Palmyra in Syria and the

Assyrian towns in Iraq. It has witnessed the tragic destruction of the Old Souks of Aleppo and Homs, along with countless ancient buildings and relics caught in the crossfire. These losses, despite their severity, are of course incomparable to the human losses – the wasted and damaged lives of innocents, and the destruction of the social fabric – but they constitute further reasons for me to write this book: to consider the paths that have led to this ordeal and to shed light on the role played by the built environment. I suggest that the failure to create architecture that can constitute a home for its users stems from a loss of identity, which in turn has causes that go deep into the psychology of our people. When we look at what is being built in the Middle East today and how it is being built, this loss of identity becomes glaringly apparent, as does the jarring disconnection between the rich heritage of the past and the empty modernism now being imported to form the present.

Grief over the violence that ISIS has perpetrated on 'innocent' ancient buildings can be contrasted with reactions towards the mass destruction of entire cities. Why is it that ancient sites mean so much to all of us? Why is a scratch on a column in Palmyra of more consequence than the demolition of an entire concrete building? Furthermore, how was it that we vandalized our own cities in Syria before war came to deliver the final blows? And how should we rebuild what has been destroyed so that it will not happen again?

In searching for answers to these questions, I have lived a certain kind of life – not, to my mind, the easiest one. In telling the story of my city and the story of my country, I also tell my own story, in so far as it is relevant. I hope that the reader will learn something from these three stories that will help to avert in other places the kind of destruction that we have had to suffer here in Syria.

Homs, June 2015

1

THE BATTLE FOR FREEDOM
One Who Lacks Cannot Give Back

Everyone in Syria has lived his war. Every day people have fought for their lives, every day has brought a bid for survival, but it is not only bodies that suffer; souls, too, go through these battles, dying a thousand times in anticipation, only to rise up wearily to face another day. Hundreds of thousands of these excruciating battles have been fought, and still are being fought, for when the drums of war are beaten no one can escape the sound. But the battles were started long before the first drum was struck.

Actual war often comes after a series of minor hidden wars. Although they are considered less bloody and destructive, these minor wars – these parries against profiteering officials; these responses to intolerable living conditions – are still bitter, because they are suffered in silence and solitude: no newspaper will write about them, no TV channel will show interest in them, and no organization will offer readiness to help.

People try to fight these minor wars one by one, but they lose most of them until the 'actual' war begins in full force. The strange thing is that most people – including those who were fighting all along – are still surprised, as if war had caught them off guard.

The laws of the universe have made no exception for this Syrian war, which flared up when social diseases had settled in the alley-ways and on the rooftops. Vicious viruses of greed, corruption, dis-honesty and ignorance had infiltrated the immune system of the communities and made clear highways for every imaginable – and sometimes unimaginable – form of torture. So it has been in this country for four years or more.

The legitimate question 'why did this happen' has received all kinds of rhetorical answers and has inspired all sorts of conflicts. We have seen mutual blame being laid by two parties who act as if they have arrived at the scene of a bloody football match, only to discover that each player is a team on his own and that no one is suffering more than the ball.

Why did this happen? We will look at the answers in the pages of this book. Many people simply wish things would 'go back to the way they were'. I have heard this phrase many times, from very different kinds of people, and each time I hear it I think, why would anyone support a process of massive change, then simply – and very late in the day – regret the destructive repercussions and want things to go back to the way they were! Even if the individual wasn't personally involved in the process of change, why would he or she want things simply to be as they were: why not wish for better, why settle for the state of instability that brought us here in the first place? This gives me the feeling that we haven't learned any lessons from all that has happened; that we have never reflected on anything, or tried to relate cause and effect.

The habit of dreaming about a tomorrow-matching-yesterday brings to mind a short story. A poor villager lived with his wife in a shabby one-room shed. The woman continually complained about her cramped conditions and nagged her husband to provide a better home. Although he lacked money, this man didn't lack wit. One day he brought his wife what he called a gift: a goat to live inside their tiny room with them. As it was cold outside, the woman reluctantly acknowledged that they had to bring the goat indoors. After a few days the man brought another 'gift': this time it was a hen. The same story was repeated over the next few weeks; each time a new animal was brought into the ever more suffocating room ... until, one day, the man decided to move all the animals out and get rid of them once and for all. The woman couldn't have been happier. She showered her husband with thanks and contemplated with great contentment the spacious home that was now theirs. In the case of Syria, however, there is no such easy way back to things as they used to be ... for the shabby little room has been destroyed.

Still, I could never wish for things to go back to the way they were; to an era when I – like hundreds of thousands of disoriented young people – felt stuck in time and space, waiting for nothing to happen; waiting as everybody, consciously or unconsciously, was waiting. I was jailed behind the bars of nothingness.

While Homs – the place where I was born and raised – is the third biggest city in Syria, it always seemed to me like a neglected village, where nothing much happened and every day was pretty much the same. I used to hate holidays and weekends because the 'leisure facilities' were so inadequate that there wasn't a single place my children could have a decent experience: no functional public parks, no cultural centres open to the public in a systematic or organized way, no zoos, no amusement parks; and, even if those places had existed, there would have been no exciting activities, no safety measures, no tasteful or memorable architecture.

In those days, my children and I would pick up other people's empty potato chip bags and plastic bottles just to clear our space on the patches of greenery beside the road where people, lacking other options, would have their picnics. No one else was motivated enough by our actions to pick up even a tissue; nevertheless, I was convinced that I was teaching my children a lesson. I insisted on telling them all about the stipulated heights and details of pavements and street planning. I didn't want them to grow up and think their surroundings were acceptable the way they were, and I didn't want them to shrug off the ugliness, even if its existence would never be their fault.

Every walk in the city was a struggle for me. Of course, this was not the most important concern in a country where, if you arrested the thief who was trying to rob you, you were as likely to end up in jail as the thief. Favouritism and bribes were the only system, and they functioned smoothly because the vast majority of people were reconciled to the fact that this was the way things were. Every sector had its own mafia, its own game rules, and very few were unwilling to participate. Even fewer were willing to fight, since the battle could take a lifetime. So the majority chose one of two paths: either the way out, to the Gulf or the West, or the way in, to corruption and degradation.

It is only natural for immorality to shout louder than its opposites, just as the dark spot shouts above the white cloth on the table. But when immorality prevails and life loses its equilibrium, as it has done in Syria, things can only get worse.

The future, for most Syrians, has become a word of one syllable: 'mine'. It means having a home, a car, a family, a steady income. In the current matchbox world, ideals, dreams and public spirit are all considered laughable; you may be accused of being crazy, suffering from obsessive-compulsive disorder or behaving like an elitist snob if you try to maintain standards. 'Stop acting as though you were raised abroad!' snapped a friend, when I refused to sit in a smoke-filled room. I fought with every taxi driver in the city over speed limits, crossing red lights, smoking in the car. Demanding such rights was considered a pretentious luxury, and laws that had once been passed to protect those rights were no longer enforced.

At that time I didn't dream of owning a home. Why would I run after that carrot with my tongue on the floor just to live my old age in peace? I simply wanted – as innocent young people still want – to be somebody, to do something, but without deviousness or force. But that was, and still is, too much to ask.

Wondering about the causes of this war reminds me of a lung cancer patient wondering about the cause of his disease, when he has been a couch potato all his life, smoking heavily, drinking to excess and gorging on junk food. No matter how diverse and serious the external threats, a 'healthy' country would not fall apart in the face of a crisis, and, no matter how corrupt and ruthless the governing powers, a 'healthy' people would not eat each other up like savages.

There is a saying that 'money and power don't change people: they just show them as they truly are'. War does exactly the same. Ignorance mixed with injustice makes for a deadly cocktail. In Syria this mixture is our daily dose, and the glass has been filling up over time. One can sense it in almost every aspect of people's lives. And the cost inflicted on the built environment has played a major role in heightening and perpetuating what has turned into a major catastrophe.

When, at the age of 17, I began to study architecture at the city college in Homs, I became acquainted with a different world, through the pictures of international projects in books and magazines. Our professors urged us to draw inspiration from what we observed in those images. I remember our very first project as freshman students: we were asked to design a house and to provide sketches of its exterior. Our professors recommended sources of inspiration ranging from the American home styles of New England and Cape Cod to illustrations from randomly chosen library books. They made no distinction between the styles; they just showed us images completely detached from our own reality.

This approach was cemented during our five years of study. Professors would introduce us to a type of building but give us only a name and short description. We were supposed to do some research on its functional program via very limited resources, confined to a few shelves of the college library. The internet was not available, so we had to rely on our own initiative.

I had a friend whose sister used to send him a monthly architectural magazine from Italy, where she lived, and I would buy a copy from him, then circulate it among other students to share the educational benefits. On this monthly supply I fed my inspiration without any understanding of the implications of what I was receiving, and without any reading of the historical, philosophical or intellectual background. It was like eating bits and pieces from all over the world, blindfold, and trying to understand the art of cookery.

The funny thing was that the educational system of the architecture school was based on promoting the most theatrical of shapes, yet with a very rigid understanding of the functional program. We were taught that there were very few ways to 'go around' the function of a building. Professors wouldn't accept any suggested functional solutions or zoning other than the settings they already had in mind. Any attempt to break with these would be met with a failing grade.

To satisfy their teachers, some students would copy the outlines of celebrated international projects from magazines. The professors seemed to have no idea that this was happening, since very few of them showed any signs of caring enough to take a good look at the wider architectural world or to familiarize themselves with its icons. If they did know about any new developments, it was almost certain their interest would be confined only to the images they saw and not to any engineering or other challenges that might have been overcome to reach the final result, let alone any criticism or theory behind the work.

Students were also set the task of 'solving' interiors according to the set program. Often a student would secretly trace the outlines of a successful building found in a publication, then tweak the insides in order to fit the pre-set areas and functions required by the professors. If the student then shared this with others, the sharing had to be performed in secret, since it was considered to be cheating and that had its consequences. I was never a fan of the process. A few others and I preferred to design our own solutions, but that meant a lot more work and lower grades.

In effect, we were practising a fake freedom. We were free to draw inspiration, free to use free forms, free to think as we wished, with absolutely no constraints, but the teaching program could not be changed.

On the other hand, the professors really did have freedom when they wanted it. In the absence of genuine standards, and respect for knowledge as something objective, they were free to evaluate as they pleased, with no clear rules to define the process. In the students' absence, their projects were 'sentenced' and, with a sprinkle of administrative corruption, luck was always the master of the situation. How does the judge feel today? Does he like curves at the moment, or is it angles? Does he have anything against this particular student, or has another already received special treatment? Is this student a relative, or does he have a family connection with an influential official? Is this student wealthy, or is she pretty? Ignorance and injustice were practised freely, to produce the chosen architects of tomorrow who would build our city – a city that was deteriorating rapidly in the hands of its governors and residents.

Typically, the governor of a Syrian city would come from elsewhere, with the mayor – usually one of the city's well-known figures, and preferably someone from the upper class – in charge of the built environment. These were not written laws, just the inescapable rules of the game. Yet controlling the built environment is a huge responsibility: the face of a city governs the daily routines of its people and all that pertains to their way of life. Nonetheless, it has become a lucrative source of income for unscrupulous alliances who construct the city for their personal benefit and without regard for its inhabitants.

As young architects approaching graduation we used to encounter our senior colleagues and observe the blatant despair on their features, their sloping defeated shoulders, their low-pitched voices, and their eyes dried of hope as they warned us of the major disappointments in store for us. It always took the spring out of our step so that we went forward haltingly, our 'perfect' projects rolled up in our hands.

I remember one senior friend trying to 'prepare' me for the ugly truth, telling me what I wasn't told at college: that everything I was designing and dreaming about was a total waste of time. 'Look around you' was a sentence enough to wake anyone from his illusions. In the 'real world', it was the established powers, led by the governor and the mayoral offices, who decided the shape of architecture; it was not the classical theories of the art, and certainly not the 'nonsense' theories of deconstruction and post-modernism that seemed to be all the rage in the West.

This was what our predecessors were trying to warn us about. They were trying to explain to us how hard we would fall when we leapt from our ivory tower onto a cracked desk in the back of an empty 50-square-foot room. As like as not there would be no job for us to do, except for signing a paper every now and then, drinking tea and coffee while waiting for the boss to leave, and then sneaking out afterwards. There were no serious practices to learn from; only a bunch of small offices, which at best would need a draughtsman. There was no scope for design or improvement: the cake had already been sliced up and allocated to the waiting jaws.

We were so detached from reality that no one among the staff cared to enlighten us. How could they explain to us that none of what we were learning was ever going to see the light of day? How could they tell us that we should forget all about architecture and design once we graduated, either to be employed in some corrupt governmental administrative sector or to enter into some unsatisfactory contract with a union, where our only mission would be to negotiate over the 'leftovers'? Simply put, there was no place for dreams, work or dedication; there was only a mob collaborating to make business from the streets, infrastructure and buildings of the city, by monitoring, controlling and directing their endeavours in the most greedy and tasteless manner.

Nothing mattered to these people except profit. The whole destiny of the built environment, and consequently of people's lives, was sucked up to the very last drop. A young enthusiast with architectural fantasies had no place at all in such a system. Watching your predecessors, you felt like a droplet of water in a river taking the journey of your life towards the blue sea, only to hear a water-fall getting louder and louder, and to feel the current getting stronger and faster, until you reached the edge where your friends had gone ahead of you, dropping on the knife-sharp rocks and shat-tering into spray. My senior friends took this ride: some left the country for the Gulf, where they complained bitterly of loneliness and homesickness, longing for the day when they had saved enough money to return to the place that had rejected them.

After graduation I officially became an architect. I had no illu-sions of being the next Zaha Hadid, or even of trying to make my city a better place. Nevertheless, hope is blind and always manages to find its way to the human heart, mine included. The Syrian gov-ernment automatically signs up new graduates of certain speciali-ties at its institutions. The graduates then have the freedom to either accept or decline, though in fact very few decline such an offer, unless they are leaving the country, and even then they might still find a way to 'save their seat' just in case.

As an architect – and one who had not exploited any influential contacts or paid any bribes – I was assigned to a miserable office, where I did nothing all day, along with others doing nothing all day: just dozing, eating, then hurrying back home. I started to bring in a book to read, though that made me look weird.

After a while I applied to be moved to the architectural office at the administrative headquarters of the city university. Although its name suggests that the office was related to architecture, the reality was that there was very little architectural practice in evidence there. Feverishly I watched the hours and minutes of my day go by, captive to this non-existent job. I wanted to quit, but my husband urged me to stay a few more months and make the most of the experience. His advice was not to leave something until I was aware of all of its dimensions: with all the downs there must be ups, he reckoned, and I should stay until I figured them out. So I stayed on and meanwhile applied to study for a Master's degree.

While most of the senior employees at the institution formed closed inner circles conspiring to sew up deals with independent businessmen and influential public figures or officials, I spent the long hours waiting for someone to assign me a job. Finally my boss, who was a professor of civil engineering and trying to introduce whatever reforms he thought were possible, gave me the task of designing furniture for some offices and dormitories at the university. I was thrilled to be given this opportunity. I pored over sketches and drafts the minute I arrived at my workplace, though that made me the monkey in the zoo performing for the curious visitors. Indeed, my employers – whose daily routine was to check in, have a 'divine' cup of coffee that no one would dare to interrupt, chat for an hour or so, do some of the accumulated paperwork and then find a way to go home early – started to circle around my desk with unconcealed amazement on their faces, asking me curiously what I was doing so early in the morning. They couldn't wrap their heads around the idea that someone would actually start work instantly, without the prolonged morning routine, and would go on sketching so seriously. They thought I was mad.

I interviewed the head of the department that had requested the furniture. The office items were to go into a suite of spacious rooms. It was hardly surprising that a Syrian governmental institution would contain such generous office accommodation, since space was seldom an issue, no official decision-making ever taking into account concerns such as environment or footprint. On the other hand, with typical inconsistency and disregard for the 'lower ranks', the furniture for the dorms had to be minimalist in view of the relatively meagre budget and – in this case – lack of space. Five or six students were to be crammed into each room, with a shared bathroom at the end of the hallway (when I visited the dorms for the first and last time, I almost fainted from the smell). The poor finish and the lack of maintenance had taken its toll on everything and everyone, including the hapless students, who did not have enough space for storage and whose mini kitchens and bathrooms were in very bad condition. Looking back at my designs for the office and dormitory furniture, I realize that they weren't as convincing as they should have been, but nonetheless I tried my best to come up with solutions that might ease the lives of the students and offer them utilities that would be respectful of the necessities of life. After submitting my designs, I did not hear any feedback. They were evidently rejected, but no one ever told me so or the reason why. However, in a later interview with the principal, he expressed his discomfort and astonishment at the fact that my table design had 'showed his legs'; the man wanted a fortress to hole up behind!

I spent nearly eleven months of my life in that office, and that was enough 'experience' for me. To the complete bewilderment and shock of every employee I knew, and some I didn't, I submitted my resignation. My colleagues couldn't believe my stupidity in leaving such easy money. Many of them recommended a mitigating proce-dure, which was to leave temporarily without totally terminating my 'chance'. In order to fire an employee from the public sector, any boss would need an official decision from the ministry. In addition, a steady income after retirement in a country where opportunities for private employment are very few and limited, and health and life insurance do not exist, made my decision look very reckless. However, I never regretted the decision. At the time all I wanted was to break free from the atmosphere of laziness, dishonest competi-tion and rampant corruption. I chose the way of study and research: I wanted to find answers to the increasing number of questions in my mind; I wanted to find keys to the heavy shackles that had been put on me, though I couldn't figure out how, why or by whom.

Freedom is a word with many implications. For some it is a great taboo; for others it is a call for liberty without limitation. In Syria today, in this land of conflicts and struggles, one party may see freedom as the symbol of a 'great treason', while another may believe it to be the catchword for the new 'unbeatable courageous action of the twenty-first century'. Although it would be helpful if it was an agreed idea like any moral concept, such as honesty, generosity or courage, freedom ranges between many poles. Does it protect our rights, or our duties? Is it a positive concept, telling us to enhance our powers, or a negative one, telling us to protect our space? Is it the stuff of an American marketing campaign, or a threat that sends the fearful scuttling to the barbaric jungle of the ignorant? 'My freedom ends when yours begins' is no longer common ground, because those very limits are no longer defined or agreed upon.

Freedom has become so unfree. For many it represents no more than a green light to sound off on social media, disrespecting anything and anyone as much as they like. Others have heard throats cry 'Freedom', as in the movie *Braveheart*, and as on the astonished streets of Homs – one of the first cities to witness this phenomenon. With this word we were thrown into the 'war of the century', as it has been called: families have been shattered, much blood has been shed, and a whole country has entered through a dark door into the unknown. Differences, which are the key to freedom, are forbidden, we discovered, in the battle for freedom.

Naturally, I was one of the countless people who found themselves in the middle of this battle without asking for it. When demonstrations started – at first timid and nervous, like a little kid taking his first steps into the great outdoors beyond the closed doors of his home – people would go out after Friday prayers, the time when the only regular crowds are assembled. Immediately, the stratified society of Homs separated into its classes, like water and oil: social groups marked their boundaries, while any 'lost molecules' were sentenced to rejection or worse.

I was one of those lost molecules, since I did not automatically take a side or follow what should have been my pre-set stance.

While my seat was reserved in the rows of the 'Sunni + Homsi + middle-class + prosperous + educated', where one automatically has a ready-made opinion on the events of the day, I was unlucky (or lucky) in that I had a 'different' mind.

I was raised by raising my two children. I came to believe that I should always evaluate the behaviour and not the person, and that I should check reports for myself and not take others' words for granted. But this meant that in every discussion I constantly appeared to be spraying water on a flame. This made a lot of those who were around me furious, albeit in a way that I was expecting, since I was at the time reading about stereotyping and what it means for someone to break with group consensus. I was perfectly aware of the consequences, but nonetheless spoke my mind, condemning what I believed to be wrong behaviour from (at the time) both parties. I didn't take sides, and so I was socially ostracized.

It was only the beginning of numerous battles to come for all of us; battles in which everybody is a loser, in which 'freedom' is no longer an issue or a demand. The cry, which used to break out in the small alleyways of Homs only to disappear after a few minutes, sadly along with more and more young people each time, disappeared too. Those who lack something cannot give back. Very few realized at the time that there would be very hard lessons to be learned, in the most bitter of ways, before real freedom could ever find its way to us.

2

THE BATTLE OF OLD HOMS
The Defeat of the Old by the New

There is an inescapable correspondence between the architecture of a place and the character of the community that has settled there. Our architecture tells the story of who we are. The people who construct and use a building are therefore not the only contributors to it; those who may never enter it and those who simply pass it by may equally contribute to its formation, because they are part of the social reality that led to its creation.

Before the war, Syrian communities were united by a shared approach to life. They were generally fairly tolerant and were historically used to variety, accommodating a wide range of beliefs, origins, customs, goods, even climates and food. This variety, in fact, inspired tolerance on a level that many other societies with similar economic and political systems almost certainly lacked. For instance, Syrian communities exhibited no real discrimination concerning the role and rights of women, or the coexistence of different religions, family structures and ways of life. Generally speaking, women in Syria have not had to fight to get an education or to be properly represented in the fields of politics and culture. They have contributed to their communities without the need for struggle and, surprisingly enough, this is as true of the most remote village communities as it is of the city, regardless of social and economic status.

The same applies to freedom of belief, which has been the greatest casualty in the recent crisis. People accepted the challenge of other ways of life, lived peacefully for centuries with diverse beliefs and customs, and were even sufficiently free from taboos that they could discuss their differences comfortably. This was not due to any political decision or imposed plan: in my view, it was a natural outcome of the sheer variety of life made available by free movement and trade.

This description now seems utopian, set beside the current fashion for slaughtering and beheading. It is enough to scan through social media pages to witness an unprecedented race towards sectarian hatred. The cheering for blood and death, as at some Roman games, scandalously contradicts the portrait I have given. How does a long-established peace degenerate into civil war, and how do modern and hitherto progressive communities collapse from a state of civilization to a nightmare of animal carnage?

The built environment is not irrelevant to that question. Architecture offers a mirror to a community, and in that mirror we can see what is wrong and also find hints as to how to put it right. I will start from my city of Homs. Although each city has its peculiarities, there are also broad similarities that make it fair to generalize. In this sense, Homs is not a special case: its tale is the tale of all Syrian cities.

The city was built in ancient times on the banks of the Orontes River, which is dear to all citizens of Homs as Al-Asi, meaning 'the disobedient', because it flows against gravity from south to north. The city is situated in central-western Syria. The land is fairly flat but spread over a vast volcanic hill, which offers rich soil for agriculture and an eminent building material of durable black basalt. Because of its dependence on agriculture, Homs cannot claim that trade is one of its strongest points – but there are other reasons for this, to which I will return.

Damascus is so famous for its white jasmine that the flower is known as Damascene jasmine, but nonetheless it seems to flourish even better in Homs's quiet streets, dangling over fences at every corner, offering a remarkable freshness to our morning walks. This freshness used to be enhanced by the breeze, since an opening between mountains on the west side of the city allowed the wind to sweep across the plateau. Thus, air currents from the sea made summers in Homs more bearable than in other Syrian cities. This wind also left its mark on the trees, which are all bent towards the east. You always know that you have entered Homs when you see these bent trees along the roadside.

Since the beginning of its long history, Homs has been the stage for brutal battles, beginning with the Battle of Kadesh in 1274 BC, the largest chariot battle in history, fought between Egyptians and Hittites, and probably concluding in a draw – as lethal and as pointless as our conflicts today. Although Homs has had its golden days, it has also endured systematic deterioration and the constant removal of important and ancient features, with irreversible consequences. Thus, the Ottomans demolished the city wall and five of its seven gates in the eighteenth century, leaving the town vulnerable to the raids of nomads.

Such abuses have been repeated during the ensuing two centuries. One particularly painful event was the building of a petrol refinery in the 1960s, very close to residential areas on the west side, the side from which the prevailing wind blows across the city, thereby bringing pollution together with a distinctly unpleasant smell. A composting factory and a sugar factory were also built in the same area, adding to the pollution. Once famous for its fair weather, Homs is now notorious for its dirty air, dusty streets and noxious smell.

It is also known for its two clock towers, which stand at either end of a street less than a kilometre long. These clock towers carry a great deal of significance for Homsis and are the only major landmarks in the city. The 'Old Clock' marks the square of the Old Souk, while the 'New Clock' (built in 1958 through the vision and donation of Korjeyya Haddad, who, although she lived all her life in

Brazil, was originally from Homs) marks the new market square; it has also become the Homsi symbol of the 'revolution', as it is where people assembled as a substantial crowd for the first time to participate in what has become known as 'The demonstration of the square', and it is where many were shot to death in the bloodshed known as 'The carnage of the New Clock'.

The people of Homs have relied heavily on their homegrown social system, based on the hierarchy of money and power, creating a conservative and introverted community full of contradictions and social discrimination. However, they are also known for

▼ The demonstration that turned into 'The carnage of the New Clock'. The official Communications Building appears to the left and the domed Old Homs Cinema building to the rear, behind the prominent New Clock tower.

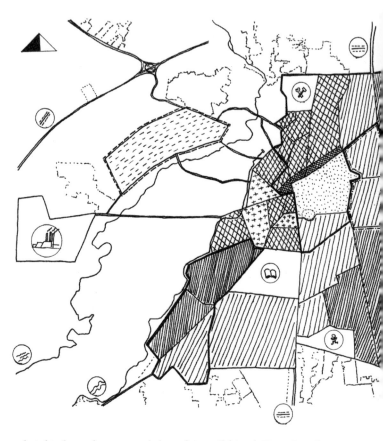

their kindness, humour and shrewdness. Although Homs is a city of over 1,200,000 people, everybody knew everybody else's whereabouts long before Facebook. The system endowed notable families with social and economic power, and hence with the lion's share of the market and the built environment. Many neighbourhoods and streets in Old Homs and the city centre are still named after major families or after characters well known in the community.

Homs consists of five sectors, categorized according to key architectural characteristics and periods. First there is Old Homs, which

◄ Map of Homs

Informal housing

Social housing

Middle-class housing

Prosperous-class housing

Old Homs

Commercial zone/Downtown

New Homs

Industrial area

Public university

Public sports complex

Petrol refinery

Irrigation canal

Orontes River

Highway

Evacuated/90% destroyed

Besieged/60% destroyed

50% destroyed

is the core of the city and the oldest part, originally built inside the ancient walls that protected the city from intruders. The old city stayed within its circumference for a very long time, despite falling into ruin. Not until the 1940s did it expand beyond the zone of its long-demolished walls. This city was surrounded by orchards that grew lushly next to the Asi River, with its irrigation canal and ancient waterwheels.

With the issuing of an Expropriation law in the 1950s, allowing the government to confiscate private property for public use, the door was opened to extensive construction outside the city boundary. What became the next city centre was extended northwards from the end of the souk and its square, forming a relatively enclosed downtown. In this sector, urbanism created a mixed-use continuation of the old city, with features of colonial architecture, such as tiled pitched roofs and narrow arched windows, later mingled with random additions that have neither identity nor architectural sense.

The third sector is comprised of the more residential neighbourhoods, containing the middle- and upper-class residences, with features ranging from the 'experimental modern' to an anti-architectural nothingness.

Next come the social housing developments that surround the city. These do not exhibit the typical features of modern slums: they are built out of cement and blocks, and have roads for cars and a proper supporting infrastructure.

Lastly comes the expansion of New Homs, built outside what remained of the green belt, separated from the city by the river but connected to it by four parallel roads. The sloping hill area is chiefly residential, with buildings from two to twelve storeys high. In view of the inefficiency of public transport and the lack of other amenities, this area is to a great extent isolated from Homs proper.

In the old city we find buildings with courtyards, built of basalt stone and squeezed back to back along the narrow twisting alleyways. Ancient churches and mosques were built in the same way, adjacent to or opposite each other. The coexistence of many religions was expressed in an urbane architecture of which peaceful settlement was the principal social characteristic. Although the buildings do not strike you as in any way exquisite, they are still unique in terms of the distinctive building material, used according to proportions and scales in which humility and harmony are the ruling principles.

The social fabric of these areas was woven according to the same principles as the architecture: mixed use, mixed origins and mixed religions – a habit of mixing that was to be treasured and is now sadly missed. It was common to hear the bells of Christian churches and the Muslim calls for prayer echoing through the streets at the same time.

Old Homs contained a living museum of ancient architecture, but its treasures were jumbled and neglected, like dusty jewels at the bottom of an abandoned drawer. Among the many precious buildings, two stood out because of their sentimental value for both Muslims and Christians: the Ottoman mosque of Khalid Ibn Al-Walid, and the holy church of St Mary. The two monuments have much in common: both of them are important to every Homsi, both suffered the same horrific destruction in the recent conflict,

▼ An area in the Al-Hamidyah neighbourhood of Old Homs commonly called 'Between-the-two-minarets'. The minaret of the older mosque on the left was built using typical black stone; its main building is submerged between the ruins of old houses. The rear façade of the Catholic church can be seen damaged in the distance.

and, most importantly, both contained something venerated as of the highest holiness.

The mosque is named after the Muslim military commander who is buried beneath it, hence Homs is aptly termed 'the city of Ibn Al-Walid'. This building contains architecture in the style of Mimar Sinan, the great architect of the Suleymaniye mosque in Istanbul. It was rebuilt in the first Mamluk style with two white

linear limestone minarets and nine overlapping silver domes. Both Christians and Muslims volunteered to work on the building, which was conceived as a shared treasure. Using the common black stones, the almost cubic block was mounted by a central dome reaching 30 metres in height, making the mosque a visual landmark that no other building surpassed until very recently.

Unlike much religious architecture, the Ibn Al-Walid mosque is not highly ornamented, either on its exterior or interior. On the contrary, serene modesty is a key characteristic. Every detail of the architecture expresses the elegance of simplicity, including the clean basalt façades with limestone window frames, the hand-wrought ironwork of the grilles on windows and fences, and the alternate black and white stripes called *Al-ablaq*, which is a typical feature of Islamic architecture in the Levant. The handiwork of these relatively simple details – whether in the cutting of stones, the soldering of metal or the framing of edges with punctured mouldings – all expresses a serene and simple love for the work.

◀ Khalid Ibn Al-Walid Mosque, its
main façade and minaret damaged.

Inside we encounter the same minimalist approach, strongly reminiscent of the Sufi state of mind that is part of the atmosphere of Homs. Many of the chief Sufi masters were born in the city, which is considered the mother of Sufism in Syria. The interior of the mosque reflects the ascetic way of life that the Sufis adopt. There are four main pillars supporting the central dome, each made from a cluster of contiguous thin white columns. The interior surfaces are off-white, leaving the Mihrab and Minbar standing out tranquilly from the plain background. A rare and priceless piece of the Minbar was looted during the terrible recent events: it was one of only two matching pieces sculpted from wood and ordered by the great Muslim leader Salah Al-Din Al-Ayyubi (known in the West as Saladin). The tomb of Khalid Ibn Al-Walid sits under a domed shrine, and two other men of great importance to Muslims lie next to him: his son Abdulrehman and the son of the caliph Omar Ibn Al-Khattab. The green metalwork of the windows is matched by the green of the wooden struts supporting the shrine's small dome, above a rectilinear white structure, penetrated with fine ornamented glazing. This work suffered severe damage in the recent fighting: its wooden dome was smashed, and the precious pieces once displayed in the rooms under its Riwaq (colonnaded section), where a one-hall museum and the Islamic theological school were located, have all been looted.

The mosque sits at the north-east end of Homs. This was originally the outer frontier of the city, but over time the city enclosed it, turning the surrounding village into a residential mixed-use area, named after the mosque as Al-Khalidiyah. An ancient cemetery ranging over different historical periods used to be situated in front of the building, but this has been replaced by a vast square with a few plinths and a green park. During the removal of the cemetery, ancient ruins were discovered. Instead of housing these in a museum, the city council merely set up, unattended, a giant lion sculpture and parts of columns at the north end of the park.

This area has been the scene of battles between Syria's official army and the opposition forces, which contain many of Homs's young people. The destruction has left the mosque with its domes punctured and one minaret half-standing in the smoke-filled air. There were rumours that the body of Khalid had been looted, but the foundations were recently investigated, revealing the presence of three bodies sheathed in lead. Unfortunately, this 'discovery' also involved massive destruction and the prolongation of a dangerous rumour that could ignite a yet more vicious civil war.

As for the Church of St Mary of the Holy Belt – in Arabic, Umm al-Zinnar – it is reportedly the oldest church ever built, going back to AD 59, though rebuilt in 1852. The church is named after the relic it is reported to house – the belt of the Virgin Mary. Every year, on the 15th of August, the belt is traditionally carried around the nearby streets to celebrate the Virgin.

The current church of black basalt is built over the old one, where Christians once took shelter from Roman persecution. Inside, a well sinks 20 metres into the earth of Homs. Outside, the architecture of the building is not that different from the ordinary houses adjacent to it. A narrow alley opens to a moderate gate of iron bars, which leads through a courtyard into the church, whose roof of pitched tiles does not rise above its surroundings. Simple embellishments frame the few arched openings on the grey block. However, the proportions of those arches and the height of the columns seem to be compressed into the constricted frame of the façade.

Entering the inside is like entering a holy cave, with black rough walls, chunky pillars and vaults going back to the Byzantine period. A few wooden benches and a small niche furnish the dark interior. The underground basement dating from the first century AD has been left untouched and is entered through the small narrow stone stairway at the back. Damage to this renowned building has been severe, though fortunately the Holy Belt has been kept safe at an undisclosed location.

If, before they were afflicted by violence, one were to have judged such buildings in terms of 'games of space' or 'accumulated powers',[1] or of aesthetic value as expressed in the term 'morality of detail',[2] one probably wouldn't find much in them. Nevertheless, they, along with the interwoven sequence of harmonious buildings that form Old Homs, somehow managed to speak to the people. Their coarse textured façades, moderate heights and low wide doors welcomed every visitor humbly into their warm and simple interiors, and for that reason they were loved, becoming – in their own way – instruments of reconciliation between communities.

➤ The Church of St Mary of the Holy Belt, its main entrance damaged.

Neither mosque nor church, nor any significant building that was in Old Homs, made a display of its importance. They didn't need to gain respect or love by showing off. However, there is a fine line between humility and indifference, and the people of Homs have now crossed that line aggressively. They have moved from a state of intellectual richness and spiritual connectivity, as symbolized in those two sacred buildings, into an immoral world of triviality and disorder. The undoing of the urban fabric has advanced hand in hand with the undoing of the moral fabric. And that is what is written in frightful scars on the face of Old Homs.

Even as a local architect, I blush to admit that I had not learned about those two buildings beyond their names until they were utterly ruined. When I was a fourth-year architecture student, our urban planning professor asked a team of ten to fifteen students, of whom I was one, to make a study of Old Homs (later on we learned that it was for the sake of his personal practice). We were asked to measure, photograph and draw sectors of the area and to present a 'current situation/proposed situation' architectural study of the façades. We were asked to document the random treatments and then to propose alternative façades, though only with regard to the surface. The idea was to impose a measure of order on the chaos. Our proposal included the stereotypical use of arches, *ablaq* and *mashrabiya* (screened oriel windows), which we were falsely taught to see as the 'secrets' of our local architecture.

I remember my impression of the old city. I was not moved by it; I thought it was unimpressive and disorganized. Although that was indeed its condition, I know today that we didn't appreciate it because we didn't understand it, and we didn't understand it because no one had taught us any different.

The old city wasn't handled as it should have been, despite the existence of a tailored building code for this part of Homs. Random and tasteless additions disgraced it everywhere. Parts of the centuries-old buildings were left crumbling; some stone houses had been removed altogether to be replaced by four- or five-storey concrete blocks. In the best case these were dressed with hideous mock-up façades of black and white stripes, in order to reflect the traditional Islamic architecture of the place (the *ablaq* cliché) and thereby to satisfy the conscience of the few who cared.

At the time of our survey, the old city was no longer able to function. Space was limited; the streets consisted of narrow, winding alleys that vehicles struggled to get into (though, even so, one found long rows of cars blocking the entrances). No one cared to plan a car parking method for the residential zone or to restore the crumbling old buildings, to tidy away the dangling electricity wires, or to repair the holes in the streets. It was as though the inhabitants were being encouraged to let go of this dysfunctional environment and to replace their humble stone houses with towering concrete blocks.

The contrast between the crumbling old and the brash new was like an insult to both, and more importantly to their inhabitants. These communities had lost their settlement and their sense of belonging, since there was no longer much in their environment to hold them together.

In the middle of this chaos and next to the residential fabric of the old city ran the Old Souk: an Ottoman-style covered market, which all the residents have worked in at one time or other. This souk enhanced the old city's micro-culture and was the artery of the life of Homs. Fabric-weaving, goldsmithing, copper-working, carving and blacksmithing were all actively engaged in, side by side. Outside the walls of this market you could have found clothing and household equipment, while across the street would be the farmers' market, with stalls selling fish and chicken all around.

Over the years new occupations gathered in the shadow of the souk: doctors' clinics and offices were housed in the upper storeys of the surrounding buildings, while new shops and travelling peddlers sat side by side at street level. The approach applied in the residential area was followed in the souk, with buildings from different architectural styles and periods – though mainly from the early twentieth-century colonial period of the French occupation of Syria – nestled next to one another.

Neglect took over the souk as it had taken over everything else, printing its marks on both body and soul, as any illness would do. To see the beauty of the place you would have had to stand away and look very hard, trying to filter out the jammed cars that turned exteriors into smoke-charred billboards covered with torn posters plastered over one another, the discordant shop signs, and the general sense of a vandalized amenity for which no one much cared. But one thing was easy to observe, and that was the vibrant life inside: the whole city lived and worked there, constantly going in and out on errands, like bees in a hive.

The rest of the city was unable to compete with the liveliness, unity and identity of the old city, where most of the 'city's sons' (as they like to call themselves) had a foothold in the form of property or business. The remaining parts were outgrowths, allowing for more spacious residential areas and scattered small businesses – dull places that sleep when the night is still young and which wake up at noon.

Instead of preserving the old part and enhancing the new, the officials in charge of our city decided to 'upgrade' its urban planning and architecture. This they did by removing large chunks of the old buildings and replacing them with ludicrous fantasies of their own. There are some memorable instances that wounded the hearts of many in Homs before the complete destruction of their city. On one occasion the town hall decreed that an open parking lot would be created for the commercial zone in the heart of the old city. As the work proceeded, passers-by would turn away in anguish at the sight.

This was neither the first time nor the last for such a 'stab'. Palaces, baths and other buildings with historic and aesthetic meaning were repeatedly replaced with dead blocks of concrete, which were of no decorative or even functional or economic merit, but simply unadaptable by-products of official ignorance. Approximately 20% of the vast 'Engineers Syndicate' building, erected right in front of the entrance to the Old Souk, was occupied, while the rest was left abandoned and in terrible condition. Another huge block – the so-called 'Ibn Al-Walid Complex' – was left unfinished, a dangerous eyesore. Both buildings were planned and executed by the military construction company, the main contractor for public projects in Syria.

On the few occasions that officials opted for preservation and restoration, this was carried out horribly. The Al-Zahrawi palace in Old Homs, for example, was acquired by the Syrian government in 1976 'due to its importance'. The palace's uniqueness stems from its side-by-side display of civilizations, which, archaeologically speaking, are normally found stacked one above the other. The Mamluk north, east and west parts of the building dating from the thirteenth century are joined to the Ottoman south, in which we see different architectural elements of various styles: Persian, Omayyad, Abbasid, Ayyubid and Mamluk, above two Byzantine basements, below which is a further layer from the first centuries of the Christian era.

However, the harmony and coherence of this beautiful building failed to inspire the official restoration team to respect it: the palace

▼ Al-Zahrawi Palace, its rear façade damaged.

was 'restored' by painting its bare black-stone walls with the brightest of colours. It wasn't enough that they chose to paint it in the first place; their choice of paint had to be as brash as possible. The semi-honeycomb Iwan (hall open to the courtyard) was painted in egg-yolk yellow, bright blue and snow white. The interiors were painted according to a naïve sense of their function, so, for example, the room where the children of the original owner used to sleep came out pale purple, like a modern kindergarten: all it lacked was a PlayStation.

Underneath the small courtyard is a water tank, with an old drinking well. However, the restoration team's stereotypical understanding of Islamic architecture didn't allow the meaning to be left unexplained, so they felt they had to add an octagonal pool with miserable furnishings. They then covered the stone ground with wooden plates fixed with long iron nails stabbed into the stone, leaving the ancient underground treasures neglected – and, luckily, forgotten. The least that can be said about this action is that it was an architectural, cultural and moral crime. The final 'artistic' touch was to name the place a museum for 'traditional culture'.

The neglected city of Homs – despite its location, size, and agricultural and industrial production, and more importantly its great human potential – has suffered greatly from the prolonged collaboration between its governors, mayors and cream-taking class. These people took turns in controlling the built environment, in most cases to the detriment of the city. Homs once had all the potential to be a city with a defined character; to be both a pleasant settlement and an attractive destination. It is without a doubt the number one city in Syria for sweets and confectionery. It even has a special kind of sweet that can only be made and eaten at dawn: a minor example, perhaps, but a marketing opportunity that, like so many others, seems not to have occurred to the officials in charge. Likewise, the Asi River could have created a special character for Homs; unfortunately, due to an ill-considered dam, it has been reduced to a small stream of dirt and rubbish, full of unpleasant insects and smells, so that environmental, social and cultural projects involving the river are now out of the question. Most importantly Homs could have become a world destination for religious and cultural tourism on account of what composes it: layers of ancient architecture stacked one above the other since before Roman times.

The reality is that urbanism and architecture in Syria belong to a single school: not modernism (which in its worst excesses is bad enough) but 'mood-anism'. The forms of the buildings are dictated by the mood of the rulers. For instance, a couple of decades ago Homs was governed by an architect who allegedly 'liked' the four-storey look, in addition to football. Accordingly, Homs was forced to put on a new face composed of chunky blocks and to be cheered for its number one football team, turning Homs once again into a Syrian Manchester (this nickname was reportedly given to Homs by an English consul in the days when the city was famous for its fine textile industry[3]).

One mayor, a notable figure of the upper crust, diverted a main road so as to save her house from the noise. She is also alleged to have spent much of the public budget on renovating the road and street furnishings around her home, in a central area of exclusive villas and apartment blocks for the wealthy, instead of addressing the neglected neighbourhoods on which the money should have been spent.

Collaboration between the mayor and the governor against the city was inevitable, and in this case it was no exception. Nonetheless, that particular governor was no ordinary one, and he turned out to be one of the most unfortunate things to have happened to Homs until the war. This official was so dictatorial, in the face of so-called 'democratic laws', that the people later nicknamed him 'Al Wali' – a reference to the olden days of Ottoman turf dictatorship. He abused the rich as well as the poor, the city as well as the surrounding villages. He is reasonably considered, in one way or another, to be one of the main reasons for the deadly conflict that ensued, having inflamed the city with his manifest injustices.

He forced harsh legislation on the dependent poor without taking any steps towards finding solutions for the dead-end buildings and infrastructure that had been imposed upon them. He was in constant unfeeling confrontation with low-income homeowners both in the city and the villages, so that building an extra room or pursuing one's own life in accordance with one's needs became virtually impossible. Armed with the prevailing

▼ The Twin Tower Hotel, as currently standing on the verge of green orchards and next to low-rise housing.

corruption and with strong connections, he was able to take control over the whole building process in Homs. Pursuing their interests many notable figures and businessmen shook their dirty hands with him, so as to be granted their shares. To win the governor's satisfaction and the rewards that flowed from his favour, those members of the community renovated some of the city's roundabouts but then adorned them with sculptures irrelevant to the city's culture.

Through manipulating the building code, one investor was granted an investment factor over seven (i.e. the number to be multiplied by the area of the property, in order to calculate the total permitted area of construction and subsequent number of storeys, was seven) – way over the usual Syrian limit of five, and by far the highest factor in the whole country. The contract was for a 32-storey twin tower hotel, to be built in orchards separating New Homs from the city, on fragile farming soil and across the main irrigation canal. It was the first building of its kind in Homs, and visible from any angle in the city. With its unprecedented height and domineering architecture it was a radical assault on the skyline. Its effects on water and soil, and its own structural stability, have not yet been tested, for the war has prevented its completion. It has been left isolated on the edge of the city, used as a firing and observation tower, sending death and destruction and constant messages of hate to the city below – a fitting representative of the modern gargantuan style.

Because the governor happened to admire towers and Dubai look-alikes, he pursued a new investment law, allowing towers to be built all over the city, including Old Homs. It was painful to witness those pin-like protrusions randomly puncturing the city, like cigarette burn marks on a tortured body. Then, due to a clash with the prime minister of the day, the law was suddenly suspended, leaving many people bankrupt. After that the building sector went utterly dead.

Even small clean industries and craft businesses such as carpet-weavers and blacksmiths were fought by the governor. Many had to close when he ordered them to relocate to a recently built industrial area outside the city, which had not been provided with the necessary infrastructure or distribution channels. The governor felt that the city should be cleansed of 'noise' and be left for shopping and living. Despite this vision, he managed to turn a blind eye to the large central factories owned by notable citizens.

The 'Homs dream' urban project was instantly renamed the 'Homs nightmare'. The aim of this initiative had been to take over shops and land at the heart of the old city and to reconstruct it, though there was no architectural vision for this whatsoever – essentially Le Corbusier's infamous proposal for Paris. The idea was to demolish the city centre, the Old Souk and the surrounding neighbourhoods, and to rebuild everything in divided zones of separate towers, the whole thing to be carried out without reference to aesthetic values. As to how the governor was going to make people let go of their properties so as to rebuild them according to the 'dream': it would be fair to say that he 'had his ways'.

The people rose up against this final insolence – an unprecedented act at the time. But none of the conflict and crisis we are currently witnessing had yet begun. The matter was swept under the carpet and everyone turned, simmering with resentment, to the new and overwhelming problems of the day.

Of course, it is always easy to blame others, but no hand can clap alone and, wherever an intractable problem arises, there have to be two sides to blame. It is often human nature to take the side of the underdog. Generally, people will support the weak against the strong, even if there is little moral difference between them. But we rarely think of those caught in the crossfire. Watching Tom and Jerry we hope cunning Jerry will get the better of powerful Tom, but in the process they both end up ruining their home, breaking things that don't belong to them and spreading destruction all around.

I also believe in the law that summarizes the outcome of any battle: the victor is always the better behaved (*al-atqa*) or the stronger (*al-aqoua*) – i.e. there is either civil law or jungle law, but nothing in between. So if we ever want to resolve this conflict and take the road to civilization, we all need to take our share of the blame.

Hence we cannot overlook the role of the Homsi upper class, who in general – with very few exceptions – instantly became 'rebels', though only in their words. Instead of supporting the poor young workers in their businesses, they kicked them out of their premises. They encouraged and even cheered at the demonstrations, but they never actually participated. The vast majority of this class, who had always laid store by their superior station in life, nevertheless rarely cared to enhance the community on which they depended for their status. On the contrary, they treated their city as a hotel where they would sleep at the end of the day or the month, while locating their work, education, leisure and shopping abroad – even if 'abroad' meant the city of Damascus. Their capital was invested neither in the city's markets nor in its appearance. Creating projects for the city's built environment was, for them, entirely out of the question. The rich in Homs, in reality, didn't have the mentality of merchants; unlike the people of Damascus and Aleppo (the two major cities before Homs) they have been accustomed to having things done for them and gaining the highest profit at the minimum risk. Despite its historical location on the Silk Road of trade, Homs has stayed pretty much an enclosed city.

Everything must come to an end, and apparently Homs is heading towards a very unfortunate one. This end has fulfilled the 'Homs dream' in destroying the old city and over 60% of its main neighbourhoods, the city centre and downtown being now almost beyond repair. Homs is the only city in the whole of blood-soaked Syria that has had its market and centre destroyed and completely shut down, while the embattled parties have danced all over the ruins, turning it into a stage of blood, hatred and wreckage. Bit by bit the city has suffered the tortures of a bloodthirsty war, starting from Baba Amr and advancing across other neighbourhoods to reach the ancient centre.

Consequently nearly all government departments, banks, businesses, clinics and the market with all its essentials have been shut down. Advancing on Old Homs the official army besieged the places where opposition troops had taken positions, in among the old buildings and narrow alleys. These places were very familiar to most of the opposition, since they were once their homes. There were people who got caught inside, having taken too long to decide whether to leave the only place they had had as a home. Some of them were Christians, and some were Muslims. These few hundred lived the life of Leningrad during the Second World War, witnessing horrible crimes and showing incredible bravery. However, those who lived to tell the tale when the siege was broken came out with extremely contradictory stories, and I learned to believe everything and nothing at the same time. In the heart of that destruction, evil and good weren't just neighbours; they were soul mates.

One of the eighteen tanks that were besieging the area used to stand just around the corner of my street and fire away. It was awful to hear the shells being fired and to wonder what happened when they landed. Teaching my son not to be uncontrollably frightened by counting the five sequenced bombs of a tank ('Four to go, three to go ...') and drawing him a map showing him how far he was from the target were desperate techniques I used to adjust to the idea that the bombardment all around would in fact spare no one.

However, the old city contained a more than two-year stock of food, clothes and money, and it offered drinking water from the old wells that still existed inside many properties. More importantly, its interwoven plan and basalt building created an impregnable fortress. The surrounding neighbourhoods built in block and cement were wiped away and entered relatively easily, but the old city was left as a perfect redoubt, with its ancient Roman tunnel network still functional beneath it. The old black stone construction was punctured and partly destroyed, but it showed a remarkable resilience. This was due not only to the organic plan and the use of stone, but also to the building techniques that had been employed. For example, during construction iron bars had been inserted into the stone to form window grilles, so to enter through a window one had to take apart a whole wall.

Layers of ancient buildings stacked one above the other were discovered during battle, effecting a sort of contingent excavation. Treasures of ancient Roman architecture were found only a few metres under people's feet. Astonishingly, some of the inhabitants of Old Homs had already known about them long before the conflict; however, they had preferred to keep the matter secret, knowing they could lose their home as a result of some untrustworthy official decree seizing a place of archaeological importance.

Underneath bleeding Homs, therefore, there lies another mummified city. Many have witnessed the tip of this ghostly underground city, with its ancient mummies and dark tunnels recalling the mysteries of the Egyptian pyramids, and its rivers flowing underground which people have known about from their old wells. No one knows how much is left and how much is ruined. It is a virgin forest of underground architecture, in which those long dead would surely not trade their positions for the life above.

Today the old city and its surroundings are beyond rescue. Its way of life has been demolished along with its buildings. People have lost their homes, their furniture, their clothes, even their photos. They have lost their jobs, their churches, mosques and medical facilities. Above all, people have lost each other. The love and harmony that existed between communities and religions has been shattered. The wounds that have been opened in this area are much deeper than bullet holes.

After almost four years of war, a partial agreement has been reached in Old Homs. After tens of thousands of destroyed houses, thousands of murdered civilians, millions of lost fortunes and bankrupt families, some sort of reconciliation has been achieved. The same hands that were firing guns on each other have shaken on a truce. A palpable relief greeted the news. Even if one knew that it was not over, any step towards peace was a blessing.

What we did not know was that a new rollercoaster was about to be ridden; a very complex series of emotions full of contradictions. Civilians were allowed to go back to check on their possessions – at least what was left of them. Streams of people flooded into the old city centre, remembering the last time they had set foot on their doorstep years before, everyone anticipating the results of destruction and looting. During their years away they had seen the huge columns of smoke ascending towards the sky, predicting that they were coming from where their homes had been, yet with naïve hope always tingling in their hearts.

I didn't have a home inside the old city, but my husband and I had set up an architectural studio there, and we also had a shop. My husband, my children and I joined the crowds of people, each walking carefully into what was once a 'dream'. Step by step we reached the frontier of what just a few hours before had been 'forbidden'. My eyes were taking pictures as I went: snapshots of red faces, empty staring eyes, small drops of cold sweat on tired foreheads. People walked side by side, electrifying the atmosphere with their conflicted feelings: caution, amazement, hatred, blame, triumph, relief, sadness, heartache. You could almost hear their thoughts: has my home been demolished or is it still standing? Is it wiped clean away or are there still a few 'memories' remaining? Is it inhabitable, is it safe to walk in, or might it blow up when I enter?

Every roaring sound, every stench of burning and every vision of hideousness one had experienced during those years came back, as though it was being experienced for the first time. Here's where you used to stop and talk with your friend; here are the remains of the shop where you used to buy your groceries; here's what used to be your neighbour's building. You're coming close, but nevertheless you're not able to realize it; your mind cannot process these enormous differences on such a huge scale.

I thought I knew what to expect. I expected to witness the destruction and plundering I had been living next to for years. I expected to see the surreal images of shattered concrete and twisted steel climbing to eat the horizon. I expected to visit our burnt-out studio and to find it, like any battlefield, full of sand bags and bullet cases, together with a strange mix of papers and disassembled computer remains, and nothing more. But what I didn't expect was the madness that filled the scorched air along with the dust and smoke. People were behaving like tourists, taking photos of themselves in the wreckage; some were even posing next to charred remains. Many were wandering around as if at some historic site, some crying, some laughing, I was amazed and troubled. I felt the most powerful curiosity I have ever felt in my life. I wanted to have the freedom to contemplate this massive strangeness: to paint it, picture it, film it, to fully absorb it, but this was out of the question in such a delicate situation. I walked over the shards of glass, with thousands of bullet cases replacing the small plants that used to grow next to the paved walkway.

Then, as they left again, families filled up the long main street, carrying the most inconsequential belongings. It didn't matter what they were taking back; as long as they had found something between the empty shell casings and the wreckage of their walls. Whether a broken picture frame or a gas cylinder, people were carrying little things back, saving the last bits of memory as a small torch of hope that they might one day return for good to the place that was theirs.

This process continued over a few weeks, and with each day the anger accumulated. It wasn't enough that your home had been destroyed; it began to feel like a further insult that you had to be humiliated by digging up trivial things just to remind you of who

▲ A neighbourhood in Homs reduced to rubble.

you were. Ugly situations began to occur, following the silly hope of finding a sweater, a photo frame or even a certificate. Some were surprised to find their homes safely untouched; but from these places radiated another series of crimes and acts of mutual hatred. To be delighted by finding your home, and then to be mortified again by watching it robbed and looted in front of your very eyes is an unbearable torment (literally unbearable, in some cases: there were reports of several deaths from heart attacks).

In the face of human suffering and pain, architecture tends to dissolve. When most displaced people simply want to close their eyes and open them again on their old home, planning, financing and building become insignificant. The real challenge lies in how not to offend people who are on the edge of exploding. How to deal with massive animosity between creeds that used to be neighbours, now full of antagonism and just wanting to hold onto their 'positions'. How to dare to dream of a better built environment, when the residents just want to block the holes in their walls with a nylon sheet and sleep through the night. Furthermore, what hope does architecture have in a place where Facebook is becoming the official court of judgment? How can architecture compete with this new substitute for culture? How can it find its place as a major subject for attention and discussion?

To the best of my knowledge, the Western world after the Second World War had a chance in that they had strong architectural institutions that played their part in filtering the built reality, promoting thought through publications and leading journals, through honorable universities and architectural conferences. CIAM, Expo trade shows and such collective efforts helped the European cities to recover. Of course, CIAM and the like had an agenda: they were in the business of taking advantage of the destruction in order to advance the cause of architectural modernism, often showing scant regard for historical continuity and the texture of the old cities in the course of this. But it was not only activists who took part in the process of reconstruction. There is a kind of public spirit in European democracies that enables people to take charge of their situation, to put pressure on governments, to start initiatives of their own, and thereby to recover from disasters by cooperative rebuilding. This meant that the destruction of the world wars was not final, but a stimulus to rebuilding. Those wars could be compared to earthquakes, where tectonic plates shake down to their settled positions. Our current wars, by contrast, are like being shoved over the edge of a cliff. What remains at the bottom is not something that can be easily rebuilt, since the people themselves are fleeing from it, even though rebuilding depends entirely on them. I ask myself: how can architecture close the wounds? I think it does not have a chance, which leaves us simply to watch the wounds closing by themselves, turning the city into a mass of scar tissue.

Our homes don't just contain our life earnings, they contain our memories and dreams; they stand for what we are. To destroy one's home should be taken as an equal crime to destroying one's soul. In that sense I believe that the pyramids of Egypt should no longer be considered the biggest tombs in history; the title should be given to the cities of Syria. And inside our pyramids there are mysteries greater than those in the land of Pharaohs. Questions that puzzle any architect who wishes to do something: where to start, how to heal, how to avoid being trapped in a vicious cycle of bad choices, how to respect rights, how to get away from division, how to reunite shattered parts, what to preserve and what to let go, what lessons to take and how to guarantee their application? Are we going to catch these last drops running through our fingers, or is everything gone forever?

I think of those questions, looking at the remains of this city with its wounds gaping open, and in the faces of its people I still see hatred and mutual blame.

3

THE BATTLE OF MORTAR
Traditional Ethics vs. Modern Life

It comes out of the blue in the most crowded of places and on the quietest and sunniest of days. It has a sharp whistle that sounds from afar and becomes fainter as it reaches its target. Then it lands with a heavy thud to throw its sharp knives at everyone and everything in its radius. It is the mortar missile: the missile that has taken so many innocent lives in Syria in the most cowardly of ways.

At first most people thought that their everyday lives would be restored soon: no one wanted to predict that the anguish would go on year after year. Indeed, the warring factions were soon racing to the TV channels to announce their imminent victories. But when war becomes a way of life, people and places go through different stages of adaptation. War always finds a way to be one step ahead of them, presenting new forms of torture around every corner.

Riding on the war machine, you descend one terrifying slope to find yourself immediately ascending the next. Among the worst phases for me were the period of mortar-shell 'rain fall' and the time of kidnap. These dark torments spread their black shadows over most of the Syrian cities, but in Homs they took on a different shade, for they relied on the sectarian division and hatred that had been nurtured by urban zoning.

During this multi-faceted war I have experienced, along with those who remained in Homs, the mortar revenge, when drops of death came from a clear sky onto schoolchildren, onto market shoppers, and onto residential streets. It happened after the warring factions had marked their positions above the destroyed city, forcing thousands of families to leave their homes. After the dust of the initial battles had settled, we opened our eyes to see a few remaining neighbourhoods surrounded by monstrous stacks of crumbled concrete. The ends of every street in those remaining neighbourhoods were blocked by these surreal structures gnawing at the skyline. You wouldn't (and shouldn't) stare at them for fear of upsetting the snipers hunkered down there. So people began to adapt to the ugly fact that the situation was not going to change any time soon, and that their homes were going to be reduced to rubble before their eyes.

This meant that new and unprecedented population densities formed. Huge numbers of displaced people left Homs, to be replaced by refugees coming from other parts of the country. The reduction in size of the city's inhabitable neighbourhoods from around 42 square kilometres to only 11 compelled extraordinary measures to be taken. Families had to be squeezed together in inhumane circumstances. Then, just when they had begun to wrap their heads around their new reality, the next round of hostilities would begin. In the game of pressuring the rival – or, as they called it, 'biting the fingers' – we, the civilians, were the fingers. And in Homs, in particular, we were the scapegoat for a revenge that was served hot and sweet and never cold.

Mortar attacks were never announced. I remember the day that I was introduced to this abhorrent weapon. The shouts and giggles of children at play were coming through my window, along with the tweets of sparrows, both of which had been sorely missed during the recent blood-marked battles over territory. We heard a heavy landing, as if a giant bowling ball had landed next door. It was a cruel, dead sound, without any startling crash. My window broke from the blast, and then came the sound of people running to help. I looked out and saw the children who had been playing football in the dusty street and the people who had lost their shops and been trying to make a living by selling odds and ends on the pavement – I saw them all lying dead. A shaking man was placing a blood-covered child in the boot of a car. The child wasn't moving, and the car was already full with others. When my husband rushed to help, he had to step over a brain that was lying on the pavement, having left the body of its owner on the next sidewalk.

This was the first time, but it was not to be the last. We had to re-live this scenario over and over again. Our streets, our buildings and our wounded hearts can still show where the shards have left their marks. We had to continue to go to work, our children had to go to school, because no one could tell when the war was going to be over. At that time, crossing an open street was a mission that needed courage and preparation. After a while, people were able to detect some kind of a pattern to the attacks; certain areas and hours were marked out as possible. Nevertheless the snipers liked to play with us, and every now and then they made a deceptive change.

The urban setting helped to make easy targets of crowds, as the city that already lacked playgrounds, shelters or cohesive urban planning became, over the course of war, a home for displaced people. Moreover, the new demographic distribution was based on sectarian differences and social classes, creating warring sectors that exchanged nothing with each other save losses.

As the available space decreased, people re-opened small businesses in order to make a living; schools became oversubscribed; and every abandoned bit of storage space became a valuable habitat. The square of Haj Atef – a perfect example of poor urban planning, with its oval-shaped roundabout flanked by six lanes of traffic – faced at one end the small hill where the ancient castle of Homs used to be. During the war, that end became an endless row of destroyed homes. But people opened street-stands all around: in addition to a bakery, a pharmacy, a few other small shops, a supermarket and a farmer's market that extended along the main street, there were two elementary schools.

The schools became recurrent targets for mortar attacks. The first time one hit them was an unforgettable day for many Homsis. That day, the mortar landed on a supply van standing in front of the school, where hundreds of children were trying to learn something besides hatred. The van burst into flames, the driver's smoking body sprawled in the middle of the street, and many dead lying around. The familiar strategy was to send a follow-up missile, but the shocked crowds never remembered this in time. Scared children trampled each other in panic, and frightened parents rushed to the scene. In times like these the Syrian people display their well-known compassion and empathy. Countless young men would rush each time to the deadly scene, knowing that they were risking their lives to rescue the wounded and the traumatized. You can only imagine how many more victims would have lost their lives with the severe lack of proper medical care and ambulances had it not been for these courageous people who never sought or received recognition.

I shall never forget the story told by a young man who rushed with his friend to help, and whose journey was interrupted a few feet before death. He and his friend were drawn to the site of the attack, not knowing exactly where they were heading. They told others not to go, to wait for the second missile, yet they found themselves magnetized by the dead and the dying. As the young man rushed forward, a little girl ran into his arms crying. The youth fell to his knees to comfort the shocked child, while his friend continued towards death, to be hit along with dozens of others by the follow-up missile.

Similar tragic stories would be told 'on the other end', in different neighbourhoods inhabited by people of a different type of 'belonging', who nonetheless shared a similar destiny to those opposing them. This vicious cycle of revenge was made possible by the curse of sectarian urbanism, which surprisingly enough has not had a long history in Homs. On the contrary, Homs had set an example to other Syrian cities through its integrated urban fabric, and it is the story of this that I want to tell.

So in what way did Homs differ from other Syrian cities, and why did it encounter a 'special' destiny? What made sectarianism so obvious and acute there, so as to lead in the end to civil war, in addition to one of the largest shares of destruction in Syria? Above all, why was the peaceful coexistence that had been lived behind those black stone walls exchanged for mass destruction?

These questions may be answered by examining the social fabric in Homs in the recent past, right before the ignition of the conflicts.[1] Despite its considerable area, Homs always felt more like a large village. In its recent past it was composed of several neighbourhoods that displayed distinctive characters based on social class, creed and economic power. These were surrounded by a green belt of orchards, and further out the residential clusters that formed the rural communities. These distinctive groupings did not differ much in appearance; on the contrary, buildings, homes, clothing and so on were strikingly similar. Differentiation could only be made through talk.

Long before social media, the Homsi community invented the 'Time Line and Walls', whereby a brief chance encounter in the street would be the occasion for the fastest 'download' process between one person and another. They would exchange news, family history and any other updates in the blink of an eye, then equably resume their paths. They enjoyed weddings and other social events mostly for the sake of their gossip-worthiness. At the same time, social prejudice and power of control between and within the different micro-communities depended on a hierarchy that gave certain wealthy Sunni Muslim and Christian families higher ranking.

Despite these established hierarchies, Homs was never a city that betrayed openly the distinctions between its native citizens. There would be no real way of guessing a person's status from the look of his home or his lifestyle. It is useful to compare Homs in this respect to Damascus, which also lived through the tortures of mortar bombing, though on completely different grounds. The conflict in Damascus didn't quite take a sectarian shape, nor was the targeting of civilians there based on revenge. The conflict was, rather, about putting pressure on the ruling authorities. Damascus differs from Homs not only architecturally and demographically but also psychologically, and this fact expresses itself in different types of economy and different kinds of urbanism and architecture.

A typical Damascene is a 'poker player', sharp-tongued but also a master of smooth weasel words, always cynical and of a strong character. Meeting you he will constantly probe; he will shake you a little bit at first to see what you are made of, and then he will continue to administer small pushes to see if he can knock you off your feet and laugh at you. His pushing depends on your reaction and he never directly confronts; nor, however, does he turn his back. He is always weighing up his prey to acquire the upper hand. As the common proverb has it: 'a hair off the pig's behind is gain.' In other words, he wants to take every meagre advantage.

By contrast the typical Homsi is someone who is called, though mistakenly, 'simple'; for he is mostly peaceful, not seeking to prove himself through the other's defeat. He likes humour, and doesn't mind laughing at himself. Hence many Syrian jokes rotate around Homs. His Achilles heel is that he talks too much and observes others too often, and from those superficial observations judges good and bad, beautiful and ugly, success and failure. So he becomes narrow-minded, and has little ambition or motivation to work. His feelings are easily manipulated, but on the other hand he is very hard to lead, because he relies on his blurred judgment of what and who is around, and considers the spread of something to be a measure of its correctness, even if it is logically wrong or ethically unjust.

Homs and Damascus have in common that they have experienced an influx of newcomers, leading to urban sprawl. However, the form and extent of this expansion, and the reaction to it, have been significantly different, not only because one is a capital city and the other merely a major city, but also because of typology, demography and the stereotypical mental differences described.

Old Homs was essentially formed of Muslim and Christian city-dwellers. It was a small city behind a protecting wall, with a history of harmonious coexistence imprinted on every stone and in every corner. Living undivided, Muslims and Christians shared every-thing – house walls, shops, alleys; even a church/mosque. The Great Mosque in Homs is a multi-layered building, and a true example of coherent living. In ancient times it was a Temple of the Sun, but it became a church when Christianity emerged from underground. Half of it was later sold to Muslims while the other half stayed as a church, until the building was damaged by an earthquake in 1157. Afterwards, it was rebuilt as the Great Noori mosque, in the heart of the Old Souk, where Muslim and Christian neighbours lived, worked and worshipped together. Of course, there is no need to state the obvious regarding the destiny of all this now. Nevertheless – and before the final destruction of such an inspiring fabric – many phases of deterioration had affected the coherence of both the city and its society. Urban and architectural vandalism, along with divi-sive sectarianism, corruption and narrow-mindedness, all dragged Homs down to rock bottom.

With its flat fertile land, lush orchards and flowing river, Homs offered an open invitation to country-to-city migration, so various Bedouin groups began to settle around its old core, subdividing the once cohesive city. Syria has been described over the centuries as a country of 'rainbow colours', combining multiple races, lan-guages and creeds. However, in outlying areas, groupings have tended to be sharper and the 'colours' usually monochrome. With each wave of newcomers to Homs, the city expanded with growths that turned out to be tumour-like. Sunnis, Alawites, Shiites and Christians of all creeds; villagers and Bedouins – each incoming community sought a life in the prosperous city. However, closed communities cannot integrate with one another easily. Hence we saw the emergence of distinct districts defined by creed, and the settling was a false one. To have only the tip of a toe touching a city cannot be considered a settlement, and does very little good for either city or newcomer. There resulted a kind of zoned urban planning that made little room for belonging. The common experience of the city was lost; any sense of belonging dissolved at the boundaries of inward-looking groups.

To be part of the city – a 'son' of the city, as they say locally – you have to belong to the city, and the city needs to accept you. Without that, both you and the city are doomed. This was not achievable for the newcomers. Living apart, they missed out on the shared experiences that create a sense of belonging; they missed both the joy and the pain. And they were also left out of the economic cycle.

The Old Souk in Homs, for example, is not just an economic centre where trade creates money and prosperity; it is a place of constant interaction, where new encounters happen every day. Trade – either of goods made on the spot (such as artisanal crafts) or brought in from the orchards and neighbouring cities and farms – offers not just cash and deals, but new faces and mentalities, making room for more acceptance on all levels. Life in the souk, with its coherent urban setting, also compels a special code of conduct that everybody has to follow, because they know through experience that it is in the common interest. This code is based on mutual respect and love for one's neighbour. In the Old Souk, everyone had to know each other's names, greet each other at every encounter, and share businesses and benefits, simply because that is the best way to do business, and more importantly because their religions told them so. The urban configuration of the Old Souk perpetuated such an experience, which is also the accumulated wisdom of the human condition. Hence, it is no coincidence to find that all the old souks in Syrian cities share the same configuration and the same code of conduct.

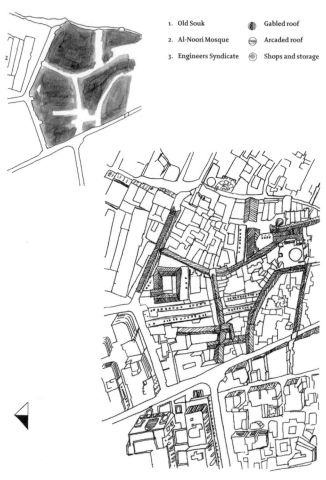

1. Old Souk   🏛 Gabled roof
2. Al-Noori Mosque   ⊜ Arcaded roof
3. Engineers Syndicate ◉ Shops and storage

▲ An overview of the Old Souk in Homs. This shows the main zone, where the souk's main routes covered by gabled roofs intersect with routes covered by arcaded roofs, all flanked by the souk's old shops and storage spaces. This was the heart of Old Homs, surrounded by key buildings such as old mosques and hammams (a few are still visible at the corners). The surrounding zones have witnessed many clearances, with old houses being replaced by new and taller blocks, some of which are shown here.

▲ Tradesmen and the interior of the arcaded section of the Old Souk in Homs.

For instance, Aleppo, the Syrian industrial capital in the north, was very famous for its markets, allegedly having the world's first 'shopping mall' – the *souq al madina*, or 'city market'. Before the recent destruction it was one of the most exquisite covered markets in the region, combining under its gabled roof and behind its stone façades an incredibly wide variety of goods. Historically, it met all the community's needs, providing even horses and other domestic animals. More importantly, what this market once presented, as a vital part of its beauty and character, was the moral aspect of trade. The merchants of Old Aleppo believed on religious grounds that you are blessed by being good to your neighbours, and that you earn your place in the community – such is what true belonging consists in. This is exactly what was perpetuated by the architectural configuration: facing and adjoining shops, a shared route under one ceiling that united them, and one sky above them all. The merchants had small chairs to sit on outside their shops once they opened in the morning. When a merchant had sold his first item, he would bring his chair inside as a sign. When another customer entered, he would then stretch his head out over his wooden counter to see if any chairs remained outside. If he saw one, he would direct the customer towards it, so as to benefit his less fortunate neighbour.

Unfortunately, the newcomers to Syria's ancient cities were mostly deprived of such an engagement: they couldn't fit in with the market or compete for a share of it. The indigenous inhabitants of those cities had learned from an early age how to be one of 'the market sons'. Those who had the necessary knowledge would pass on their moral expertise to the next generation.

Having said that, even 'the market sons' had become to a certain extent corrupted, tempted by modern lifestyles. They didn't seek to develop what they had, because that meant hard work and dedication. Easy money was available with much less effort. The alternative in Homs was employment by others. With the Expropriation Acts had come official departments, state-owned factories and the industrial awakening that reached its peak in the 1970s. The state took over properties and businesses, while offering people positions that would gain them social status and easier money. This shift from self-governing trade to secure employment was a major blow to the built-in cohesion of the city and its urban integrity. It not only meant building over expropriated productive land, it also meant more migration towards the city from the nearby villages and the abandonment of what would soon become 'old ways of life'. It changed the whole economic cycle: less agriculture, less craft and less trade. Consequently, fewer encounters with others and less variety; a loss of ethical custom and personal responsibility and more dependence on the distant state rather than the present community. And with those things came a fast-growing corruption and detachment from religious ways of life. This last change was encouraged by official policies and by the nature of the newcomers.

The practice of religion in villages and among nomadic tribes is less adjusted to modern circumstances than in the cities. This is because in cities there has long been 'enlightenment' and questioning, and the promulgation of scientific knowledge; there has also been enough money to build places of worship, whether cathedrals or mosques, which can be homes of God in which people can unite in worship and prayer. In the villages, on the other hand, extremism, introversion and the feeling of minorities being threatened have typically encountered no coherent resistance.

In Old Homs, neither Christians nor Muslims had to prove their social status through their religions; they belonged to the city, and the city embraced them through a common experience of the built environment, with their religions publicly honoured and placed at the core.[2] In Old Homs, as in all old Syrian cities, alleys embraced houses, and mosques opened their front doors to the facing doors of churches, and minarets and church towers raised their praying hands in unity above the rooftops. This way of life promoted cultivation and harmony.

These cities were *generous* cities. They offered, for free, drinking water fountains in the streets, benches to sit on, and the cool shade of trees that gave joy throughout the year with their fragrances and fruits. This generosity was a model for residents to follow; it was the womb in which a shared morality gestated. The buildings, streets and trees were not just the components of the urban environment; they were the very soul of the community, creating the faces we saw, the shops we bought from, and the shape, sound and feel of every footstep we took. In sum, such things shape our shared experience of belonging and the collective conscience of the city. These shared 'footsteps' are what make our coexistence into *one existence*.

These 'lessons' were sadly far from the reach of the newcomers who settled in new developments outside the centre. They did not enter the economic cycle that provided diversity and exchanged something more precious than money. Thus there was an evident difference between the mentality of, say, a Christian from the city and someone of the same faith who came from outside. Generally speaking, the behaviour of those who lived in the city was free from sectarian traits; they lived among their Muslim 'brothers' as fellow citizens, enjoying and endorsing the shared civil peace. They did not consider themselves a 'minority' and therefore did not seek to establish an identity by despising their mother culture, adopting Western habits or giving their children Western names – practices that were common with the Christian newcomers. These newcomers often assumed a posture of superiority to the Muslims, whom they considered to be vulgar. They thought of themselves as more cultivated, more open, more free from 'religious shackles'. In their superficial following of Western habits, they considered themselves sophisticated, dressing in imported European styles instead of in what had become for them the ridiculous patchwork of the tribe.

The truth is that this kind of inferiority complex in regard to the West is not restricted to one community in the Arab world. Failing so badly to adopt an identity after casting off the 'old' one has left us all naked – a point to which I return in the following chapters. Moreover this kind of behaviour is highly contagious, especially when the country's body is weak and unguarded. And it has found its expression in architecture. The choice of the wealthy class, empowered by the industrial boom of the 1950s, was to abandon the traditional way of building and all the accumulated knowledge contained in it. This was not a feature of Homs society alone. All Syrian communities were losing their attachments to the past, as though boarding a high-speed train while leaving their luggage at the station. The result has been a kind of universal schizophrenia.

While I was studying architecture, I had a Christian friend and we would spend our days at each other's homes, she having dinner with us while we were fasting, I praying at her place, without any feeling of disapproval from either of our families. We both felt welcome in the bosoms of our two religions; we shared the same lifestyle and accepted the same moral codes. Being so close to each other's inner circle, we became 'invisible' to relatives and family friends, and so our conversations were casual and relaxed. That is probably why a relative of my friend let slip a remark in front of me, condemning an interior she had seen as 'looking like a Muslim home', in other words not 'Western' enough and therefore to be looked down upon as vulgar. In this new unsettled world, architecture becomes a way of differentiation. And, in our disintegrating society, architecture loses its way, just as people do, acquiring new blemishes in the name of renovation and losing the humble utility of an art form that should be devoted to settlement and unity.

Careless expansion and so-called renovation has torn all the Syrian cities apart. Homs, in particular, suffered the consequences of building new suburbs based on sectarian differences, whether relating to class, creed or affluence. New Homses were built, each one for a group of non-urban newcomers from the surrounding lands. Nothing could unite these mutually antagonistic neighbourhoods. Parallel lives were already being lived, and this continued with more severity when the city died. The urban segregation turned into sectarian conflict.

Zooming in, from the urban to the architectural level, the same tale can be told: the building of concrete blocks lacking the least aesthetic sense or architectural vision denies the city its character and deprives its citizens of a congenial environment. Those new suburban Homses failed massively in social integration: indeed they enhanced social stagnation and introversion, since they created no shared identity or attachment to a place. And this architectural failing helped to inflame civil war.

Many might be tempted to see religion as the cause of the kind of conflict in which we have been embroiled. On the contrary. When religions were truly embraced within communities, it was religion that radiated affection, respect and compassion between them. And each community could establish its identity through harmonious architecture that assured it of its existence and established its settled place. Fear that one's identity is threatened leads to anger and hatred, and concrete barracks stimulate that fear, since they leave the inhabitant to his own devices, providing no shared place to belong to, but saying, on the contrary, you tell me what and with whom you are.

The traditional urbanism and architecture of our cities assured identity not by separation but by intertwining, helping to perpetuate the 'moral economy' that was tangible in the streets and the markets. This economy promoted different kinds of encounters and various styles of adaptation. It is no coincidence that the cities along the ancient Silk Road became radiant centres of civilization; not just because of the wealth accrued by trade, but also because of the openness that was taught by seeing new faces, talking different tongues, and knowing that there were *others* in the world around you, and that you were compelled by mutual interest to learn how to live with them, to do business with them and to keep together in harmony.

Trade depends on controlling human greed, but there are no guarantees that it will do this; hence the importance of religion to those ancient cities. By building temples, churches and mosques, people gave form and permanence to their faith, embedding it in the civil order and reminding all the communities of the importance of the spiritual values on which their togetherness depended. Those places of worship were located at the heart of every node of the city: at the centre, at the marketplace, in the residential neighbourhoods. They suggested something more than mutual accommodation; they suggested a higher authority that safeguarded the city and provided a guarantee of civil peace. They were part of the city's spirit; they were not affirmations of rival 'identities'. By contrast, the concrete barracks, which have no label attached to them other than the identity of their residents, have become warehouses of social disaffection.

The new extensions grew in sync with the partial and gradual removal of the old city, house by house, building by building, even tree by tree. In Homs, as in other Syrian cities, 'renovation' was accompanied by unexplained acts of removal: pulling out the generous decades-old fruit trees and replacing them with imported deciduous ones; demolishing ancient black houses and buildings with no regard for their beauty or meaning; closing main streets leading to the old city centre without providing viable replacements, and so on. At first sight, the savaging of the built environment may not convey a clear connection to civil conflict, but the truth is that each of those acts left open wounds in the hearts of the people. The official vandalism spoke to them of the government corruption that squandered their money, stole their memories, ruined their settlements, and rubbed out the marks of their shared culture.

When the built environment creates an experience of generosity and tenderness, freely offering fragrances, nourishment, cool breezes and shade in summer, and shelter from the rain and wind in winter, it becomes like a mother that cares for her children. You become a brother and a sister to your neighbours. This is what the old cities offered, with their indigenous plants and materials, in the form of an accumulated knowledge of design – the kind of knowledge that cannot be rediscovered by a single person, and that is therefore always more easily lost than gained. And this is what was ruined long before the war removed the city from the face of the earth altogether.

➤ Bab Houd in Old Homs, reduced to rubble. The open parking lot has replaced the only remaining old houses and ancient buildings that had survived the many previous clearances of the old neighbourhood. The mosque overlooking the lot is a new addition over an old mosque; the three domes did not exist before. The Castle of Homs on a small hill at the back has a few remains of demolished ancient walls vandalized by radio transmitters and communication towers.

But why couldn't the newcomers be 'adopted' by this affection-ate mother? Why were they excluded, and why did they eventually engage in stabbing her to death? I believe the answer is two-fold. Most of the newcomers were not accepted by the established society of Homs. They were not lumped together as one group, but rather they became categorized according to their religious affilia-tion, which therefore became far more of an identity label than it

had ever been before. The Alawites, for example, were originally mostly the inhabitants of mountain areas, where farming is very hard and the winter is harsh, so naturally they lacked craft skills and money, and most importantly they lacked the ability to communicate in ways that would be readily understood by their new neighbours. Due to the scarce nature of their resources – before they began to settle in cities (that is, before the industrial awakening and the expropriations) – they worked as service workers, either as renting farmers in the lands of Sunni Muslims or as helpers in the houses of wealthy city families. So when the government expropriated the landed class, exterminated feudalism, and opened factories and official departments in the cities, the Alawites had their life chance. They could free themselves from their tough circumstances and the harsh life which approximated at times to slavery. However, employment (in public departments, factories and the army) did them little good, since they maintained their isolation from economic interaction with the living city. They resided in separate districts closer to their jobs and away from the educated communities. Moreover, with their faith revolving around a philosophical notion that has virtually no link to any Abrahamic religion, they lacked the religious anchor that would engage them in regular worship and order their lives and their relationships with the people into whose traditional territory they had come. Similar stories could be told of all the various newcomers.

Along with employment came corruption, easy money, little work and much free time. Government employment is, to this day, considered tempting, especially for women (from all classes), since the law guarantees that they cannot be fired for being lazy or incompetent, and that they will still get paid at the end of every month. So, when war eventually broke out, the groupings within the whole community were already established and the religious and moral deterrent was already long lost. Stereotyping was the easiest way to comprehend the chaos. Those who were outside the cycle of city life, those who didn't suffer from having their precious built environment destroyed, those who didn't go through economic struggles in the defeated market, and those who were held accountable for official corruption since there was no one else who seemed to gain from it: they were considered enemies. Moreover they could be identified easily by the labels attached to them, and by the zones in which they lived. Battles of mutual kidnap started to occur; raids of revenge and blind killing cracked open the corpse of the city. These battles took a more monstrous, more extreme shape as they moved into the surrounding countryside, where more tightly knit groups cluster in the form of neighbouring villages that once lived in peace.

Al-Husn Castle, or Krak des Chevaliers, is an example of a location that witnessed the brutalities of such conflicts. This medieval castle rising upon a volcanic hill within a series of mountains was named a UNESCO World Heritage Site in 2006. It is considered one of the finest examples of fortified architecture in the world, with its limestone ashlars, round projecting towers and sloping glacis. My early memories of this place, 60 kilometres from the city of Homs, date from a school trip (a trip that was repeated in my days studying architecture). I couldn't get over my childhood impressions, as our teacher explained the narrow arrow slits in the thick walls, and warned us not to fall through the square holes in the floor that were used for pouring boiling oil over enemies. For me, as a young child, it was a horrifying experience, full of fear and pictures of death, so when I finally became an architecture student I couldn't get very excited about the Gothic chapel, barrel vaults and medieval frescos of this great monument. Of course, I wasn't aware of what I was missing by my lack of attention; for this monument was never going to look the same again. Significant parts of it were damaged by the severe battle between the official army and opposition troops, which was preceded by a long and bloody conflict between the two Muslim villages on the hills of Al-Husn and the

Christian villages that fill the valley – known as 'The Christians' Valley'. Dreadful crimes were committed between the valley and the hills, not in the name of religion as some might like to think, but because of political alignments that relied on identity labelling. Obviously, the question is how these labels turned into political ones, and the answer is that people were competing for a share of government funds and government employment, and all funds and privileges were in the hands of a corrupt elite. Hence the clash was fuelled by identity politics, by a shared fear for the future as well as by ignorance and injustice. All these factors might have been reduced, had architecture been able to perform its humanizing role.

▼ An overview of the inner configuration of Krak des Chevaliers showing the recent damage. These parts have undergone some hasty restoration efforts after the site of conflict moved on.

Consider the capital Damascus. Although it is witnessing a similar sequence of blood-feud events, the conflict in this, one of the oldest continuously inhabited capitals in the world, originated as a battle of country vs. city. The surrounding slums took their revenge on the 'spoiled' city residents. Mortars, booby traps and kidnappings are among the tortures that Damascus must now endure in consequence. In return, vicious air strikes blacken the once-green belt of the city. Alas, where urbanization divides people into separate sectors, they find a way to identify the enemy instantly in any conflict.

Damascus, a city whose population varies significantly between the time it goes to sleep and the time it wakes up, is a key destination for both city and country dwellers. It has also embraced newcomers from all over the world, in addition to the 'multicoloured' Syrian people. One of the many mistakes of strategic urban planning in this country was to deprive cities of civil and economic growth: thus, one city has lived from the death of the rest. 'Death' here is not too strong a word; it is a word that all Syrians would have used to describe Homs, Hama, Tartous and many others long before each one was left to meet its own completely different destiny at the outbreak of war.

When I was a young teenager, my family and I would go to visit our relatives and friends in Damascus. They all lived in the heart of the city, in towers of nine to twelve storeys, while our blocks in Homs were three to four floors at most. As in all capitals of the world, space was at a premium, and here everything was additionally cramped by the typology of the surrounding mountains. Hence Damascene homes had poky box-like rooms, awkward floorplans and tiny balconies where barely two people could fit. In Homs, by contrast, where a guest salon with a 'museum look' was a social necessity, we had spacious rooms, terraces and long balconies where guests could sit out in the summer.

I am comparing here the homes of the upper-middle classes – homes that reflected not only their occupants' lifestyles, but also their mentalities, their businesses and the urban activities on offer in their respective cities. A spacious home, half of it dedicated to guests, and half the family budget spent on entertaining and impressing them, tells you where the Homsi have placed their life axis: namely, on social status. It is also a sign of their welcoming and easy-going nature. Moreover, it shows where the community nodes are strengthened and how the social fabric is woven. Whether cause or effect of this, Homs does not have a flourishing business or cultural life, or notable public activities. The Homsi was quite content within his confined world, with its comfortable home and people coming and going. He didn't mind not having a coffee shop on every corner, or a theatre, cinema, park or library within reach. He didn't have the need or the time for such things. He also didn't mind not being rich, as long as his end-of-the-month salary allowed him to live his life 'at home' and 'with family and friends'.

For the Damascene, however, that is a naïve way of life. Unlike the Homsi, the Damascene tends to be a ruthless merchant, or a canny employer, who has had to be stronger than the rapid currents that surround him. In Damascus it is more convenient to take your guest out to dinner in one of the countless restaurants tailored to the needs of every social and economic class. In Damascus, as in Homs, the space and shape of the home is an indicator and director both of social behavior and of urbanization, in a dialectical relation of mutual influence.

The resulting mentality is also key; it dictates the shape of the built environment through economic dominance. Reportedly, large tracts of the lands of Homs were owned by Damascenes before the expropriation. Despite their wealth, many of the Homsi merchants at that time used to have simple trade agreements with the Bedouins, whereby they invested their money in cattle, but milked very little of their city's potential. Nevertheless, Homs had its golden day and wasn't always the also-ran. As I related in the last chapter, it was even supposedly referred to by an English consul in the 1870s as 'the Manchester of Syria' for its fine textiles, an industry that fought for survival through long periods of foreign governance and political struggles until, along with many others, it died.

In spite of its own story of suffering, the traditional craft economy and the Old City of Damascus were not fought over as in Homs, and the architecture of the intramural Old City was less savaged and was spared the ground-zero demolition inflicted on Homs. However, the story of the 'wannabe' Damascus that joined the modern world ahead of the other urban areas of Syria is an equally unfortunate one. As in Homs, high costs were paid and irreversible damage was inflicted.

In the second half of the nineteenth century, at the end of the 400-year-long Ottoman rule of the region then known as Greater Syria, the act of 'Turkification' that had been undertaken by the

▼ The Tekkiye Suleymaniye complex in Damascus designed by Mimar Sinan and built in Ottoman style, 1553–59. At the rear the Four Seasons Hotel can be seen.

Sultan's officials was followed by modernization efforts that spread surges of Western influences through architecture and urbanization.

Next to the major Ottoman buildings that are today considered notable landmarks, modern infrastructure and new services were built by the Turks, among them the notorious Al-Hijaz train station that was depicted in Agatha Christie's *Murder on the Orient Express*. This controversial building, combining hints of both the European

➤ Al-Hijaz train station in
Damascus, opened in 1913.

Rococo and the Islamic Ottoman, was the result of German support for an Islamic policy favoured by the Sultan, plus it reportedly affected British interests in the region. One of the immediate effects of the building was the outbreak of a Bedouin revolt in 1909, for the rail network took away the livelihood of thousands of Bedouin, while the long-term effects were observable on a much larger scale through the rapidly changing urban texture.

Unlike the Ottomans, the French who were next to occupy Syria stayed for a relatively short time (1921–1946), and yet they had a far greater effect on urbanism, architecture and social structure.[3] In 1925, for example, the French blew up the Harika ('Fire') area of the Old City of Damascus, in order to replace its ancient organic network of streets with a modern Cartesian plan. The French applied their 'Versailles' and 'Haussmannian' model to Damascus in order to expand beyond the medieval city. As with the colonial city of Orléansville, founded in Algeria in 1843, they did not respect the established heritage but simply modelled the cities they took over according to their own tastes.[4]

The regular planned grid with axis and ring roads, *étoile* and squares, new building typology, urban furniture – all were conceived as though Damascus were a part of modern France. It didn't matter if the French-style buildings were appropriate or not, as long as they served the ruling residential and military interests. The Harika 'intervention' was followed by the first master plan for Damascus and its surroundings, developed by René Danger between 1925 and 1937. The plan created many problems. For example, the perceived absence of landmarks from the intersections of streets caused the French to uproot traditional monuments and relocate them, as in the case of Maisat Mosque.[5]

To ensure the required 'stability' and the free movement of French troops and armory, French planners also cut the city off from the lush lands of Ghuta, with which it had existed in fruitful symbiosis since antiquity. And to ensure their rule, they made alterations in the fabric of the Old City. In fact, French urban planners were among the first to be enthusiastic about blowing up city streets. The Jesuit priest and Orientalist Louis Jalabert saw this as an opportunity to present 'civilized life' to the 'backward and barbaric' city of Damascus.[6] The military pilot Michel Ecochard, who worked with René Danger, was the first planner to see the city of Damascus from above, and was able to scan it using the technology of aerophotogrammetry. Bombing and building seem like contradictory words, but not for the French at the time.

Many bombardment clearances were made by Ecochard, isolating one by one the key monuments in the Old City, destroying the surrounding fabric and following the new 'modern' regulatory plan. Although the French were rejected by the Syrian people and were fought until they retreated in 1946, their imported culture tempted the affluent and was perpetuated through urbanism and architecture.[7] Despite all the urban and social problems that were created by the French intervention, Ecochard was called upon by the Syrian government in 1968 to extend Danger's plan further. 65% of the plan had been realized by 2009, resulting in infrastructure problems, urban slums, economic deficiency and social ills, leading at last to war. The aftermath of such supposed modernization is visible in the city, and it is not a pretty sight. The countless problems do not end with the traffic jams and pollution where the wide French-made streets meet the Old City alleyways, nor with the resulting messy hybrid spaces; the worst effect has been on the social fabric of this colourful society – the disaggregation of a once organic community.[8] While it must be acknowledged that (except for Harika) the intramural sector of the Old City remained untouched during the French mandate, and the original French urban planners did warn of the dangers of uncontrolled urban growth towards the green lands of Ghuta, they themselves paved the way for this with Danger's plan.

The 'Ecochard/Benshoya' master plan of 1968 for the walled city of Damascus, proposing new roads and parking lots, and the demolition of a number of residential clusters for the creation of public gardens, remained unrealized. Nevertheless, the truth is that the modern cultural life in Damascus owes much to the French urbanization. The problem with any colonial architecture is not that it brings along a foreign culture; after all, why would people have a problem with upgrading and development? The problem is that it always deliberately ignores the existence of the inhabitants of the country. It is always carried out with the same suprematist idea of *la mission civilisatrice*. Old cities under occupation were not allowed to adapt on their own and gradually to the needs of modern life. On the contrary, they were treated as *tabula rasa*, on which imported lifestyles, vehicles and equipment could be imposed without resistance. The process can be compared to an injection of growth hormones, which force a child's body into puberty, denying him the *process* of growing up, and consequently depriving him of the techniques and tools that are necessary to adapt and develop within the various phases of life. Today Damascus, like other Syrian urban areas, bears the scar-face of those multiple enforcements. And it has the heart of a child trapped in the body of an ageing but modernized lady. This child still stands lost in the dark alleys of the old city, unable to move forward or backward. For what is behind him has been lost, and he has not been taught to understand what is ahead of him.

Modern urban planning has had completely different consequences on traditional societies than it has had within its own native Western context. Those societies that were living by the religious standards of Islam as the majority religion, together with minority religions that enjoyed its protection, were forced into an alien cultural context. Their moral code was corrupted and their value system altered by the frameworks and architecture imposed from another world, without regard to the life of the place where it was to be installed. After independence, Syrian society was already on the downhill track. Despite the partial abandonment of the French lifestyle, many values had been lost, and the face of the city was forever changed. Through its own version of Communism, modern Syrian urbanization and architecture became a mixture of chaos and lost identity.

The French approach to planning in Damascus was not unique. On the contrary, Ecochard's plan for the city brings to mind Le

Corbusier's famous plan for Algiers, conceived in the wake of his master plan to demolish Paris. Le Corbusier, who was in charge of the Vichy government's planning department during the Second World War and whose work is revered in many of the architectural schools of the West and East, had proposed for the fine old city of Algiers a plan that contained massive high-rise blocks and motorways in the air to replace the alleys that had grown like vines around a human orchard with its many sects. Luckily his plan was not realized, as Ecochard's was. However, his legacy is still alive and taught both in the West and in our countries in the Middle East as a visionary ideal, rather than as an insolent assault on a subject people. The idea that architecture exists to serve people, and that it should grow in response to their living needs, seems to have been abandoned even in the West. Instead we have a new conception of the architect as someone who controls the future, and someone who has the right to herd people into zones and barracks, regardless of their wishes, and without taking any responsibility for the terrible social consequences.

During those brief visits to Damascus, I used to sense the difference between my peers and myself, not only in our definition of familiar surroundings but also in our life skills. Imprinted on my mind is the image of the view from a square window in what is commonly called 'The Russian Tower': a box-like block with a swimming pool and playground at its foot, where fair-haired Russian boys and girls would be playing (after Syria gained independence, Russia had become an important political ally). In Homs we had no such scene or atmosphere, and we were not 'skilled' as our friends in Damascus were in knowing about different nationalities and their various characters and lifestyles. Consequently, Homsi families would fear for their innocent children living in the open atmosphere of the capital, unlike the Damascene, who knew how to 'gain' more than he could lose from the embassies located in the capital and the wide variety of cultural facilities. As an ancient world trade centre, Damascus knew how to embrace 'colours', how to speak tongues and settle differences. Sectarian division was marginal: the city had hosted an intricate mix of races and beliefs throughout the ages. Its Old City narrates a similar tale to that of Homs, but its more recent urbanism and architecture are radically different. Trade was able to maintain a certain openness and diversity, reflecting the different classes of society. Even employment in Damascus, which had very similar aspects to employment in Homs, could not over-rule the 'life' that was offered by trade.

Of course, the social ills and official corruption, and underlying financial control over the market, and many more inflammatory factors that resulted in the final collapse should all be considered. They are part of the flow of money that dissected the built environment into classes and distributed people around the city according to their worth in coins. The voice of money in Damascus was much louder than the voices of morality and religion, and trade wasn't controlled by the traditional ethic: hence the shape of its built environment and of the subsequent conflicts.

In Damascus, Mount Qasioun stands defiant, rising ominously at the ends of streets. Haphazard slums cling to its rocky slopes with their bare cement and steel spikes, like a body showing you its deadly cancer. Defying you, too, are the security checkpoints shutting you off from the world's embassies and the notable rich and high officials, whose tree-lined streets run before colonial buildings standing next to modern houses, with a touch of Bauhaus detailing. Carefully clad façades contradict the 1950s finishes, and their high reflective glazing is like a row of proud faces that look out without seeing you. Rows of box-like towers with square windows and the Communist appearance of faded paint and gloomy stucco line the highways, while the air is filled with the honking of car horns. In the city centre, French-style buildings and Ottoman monuments stand face to face, smeared with black smoke and wrapped in name signs and dangling cables. At every corner a modern shop window shows you the latest fashions, next to small cafés and restaurants. The people of Homs love to go to Damascus, where they can buy things unobtainable in their local shops, eat in restaurants that never open on their streets, denounce their own 'economic futility', and visit libraries and cultural venues that they would never see back home.

Certainly, Damascus has a social class that does not exist in Homs, and that is the vanity class of high officials and 'straw-ers' (those who have their straws placed in the many holes that have been carefully punctured in the country's body in order to get drunk from its profits). In addition, naturally the size of the wealthy class in Homs cannot compete with its counterpart in the capital. But, more crucially, the wealth-holders of Homs differ in mentality from their peers in Damascus. The Homsis are more keen to keep a low profile in their actions and lifestyles; they fear display and don't dare to be so ostentatious. Whereas the middle class in both cities feel more and more pressured, compelled to austerity and threatened with disappearance, in Damascus this class is more empowered by its built environment and by the chance of small business. Homs, by contrast, is sunk in the uncreative state of mind of employees, who are riding on the hamster wheel waiting for the end of office hours, the end of the month, and the arrival of the salary.

But even in Damascus – as everywhere – things are changing. Now, in the midst of a human crisis, when people are choosing between displacement and death, the authorities are daring to attack further the urban texture that has already been ripped to shreds. Now – with ISIS closing in around the borders, heated conflicts between warring factions and an economy that is falling apart – a presidential decree has been announced to organize the unregulated informal housing areas that have grown up all around the country. This law stipulates new regulatory master plans for the indigenous zones that have used outer areas to build homes and businesses and to plant orchards and agricultural sectors. It stipulates that the occupants of these lands (owners and tenants) will 'benefit' from the yet-to-be-built mega projects that are now being planned to replace their current built environment because they will be given shares, substitute housing and a sum of money as 'rent exchange' to use in their search for temporary housing until their new Eden is ready. And there are more temptations: their properties' value will of course escalate significantly due to the new regulations. They will become 'millionaires' ... 'when the project is ready'.

Today, in these critical times, when hundreds of thousands of people are throwing themselves and their families into the middle of the sea, when Syrian societies are living through Armageddon, the government chooses to execute its 'regulatory' plan. It was already a luxury to have a place that could protect you and your family from the madness of the open sky. Now citizens – such as those barely surviving in the informal area of South Al-Mazza in Damascus – have been given an ultimatum: to evacuate their home of a lifetime to go and search for a new one, in between the mortar missiles and the front lines.

The government has announced that Damascus 'is not an agricultural or industrial city; it is a capital for housing, services and tourism', so these occupants should not be mad or sad at losing their only source of income, whether it was a small farm, a craft shop or a mini food supplier. This, despite the fact that there is enormous pressure on the retail market, where 'secure areas' are as rare as vacant places. And despite the paralyzed construction sector that has lost its building materials along with its labour.

According to the officials, this should be viewed as 'a once-in-a-lifetime chance'. Towers will be built in place of shabby housing and unnecessary greenery; modern markets and shopping malls will replace workshops and small businesses. So a butcher, for example, can finally be relieved from exhaustion and sell clothes at Zara. Not a single concrete block has so far been placed either for substitute housing or for any other dream project, but the government assures its citizens: 'The project will go on.' It has been given the friendly codename 'Project 66'. One more 6 and they can dial the right number.

In considering the two examples of Homs and Damascus, I have tried to show how the social dysfunction that finally erupted as civil war has been enhanced, perpetuated and maintained through the built environment. Likewise, trade fuelled by local production, controlled by moral codes and sustained by religious value systems is also maintained through the built environment. If one lesson can be learned from the conflicts we are experiencing in Syria – although there is far more than one lesson to be learned – it is that architecture is much more powerful than one might like to think. One could say that architecture is the reflection of human settlement, but also that human settlement is the reflection of architecture. A table set for two to dine together is surely more inviting and more inspiring when it comes to sharing, and it promises a far better experience than dining alone. The shape, size and organization of the tableware also has a crucial role in shaping experience and establishing rules. Of course, I am not claiming that the manifold complications of this war are simply the outcome of a decayed built environment and a shaken social structure. But they are significant factors, and the heuristics of the built environment are key to avoiding the terrible climax that we have suffered. As my husband once told me: if someone wishes to understand fully what is happening in Syria, he has to look at each place, each node, as a piece of a jigsaw puzzle, which will only make sense when the whole thing has been assembled. Putting Syria back together is what I am trying, in imagination, to do.

4

THE BATTLE OF BABA AMR
Social Fabric as a Foundation for Urban Design

After Dar'aa, a city in the south of Syria, Baba Amr was among the first to rise up against the governing authorities. Protest marches would go out from its mosques after every Friday prayer, a practice soon taken up by other neighbourhoods in Homs. These demonstrations were first converted to armed conflict in Baba Amr, turning the area into a backdrop for extreme violence, eventually to be entirely destroyed. Since then, the two little words 'Baba Amr' have become a metonym for either unprecedented courage or high treason, depending upon whose side you are on.

Baba Amr was once a small village on the periphery of Homs. Before the 1950s the land belonged to two main feudal landlords. Then the government, applying its Expropriation Act, took over most of the land, calling it 'emir land'. Under the slogan 'The land belongs to the one who works it', the government became a buffer between the actual owners and their previous tenant farmers, who were now granted exclusive rights of use. Meanwhile the government could sell, buy and rent out the land without actually owning the property, which was kept officially registered in the names of the original owners, who were nevertheless prohibited from using it.

The fertile, spacious lands of Baba Amr, which are only two or three kilometres from the city centre, became a destination for people migrating from the surrounding villages, who in turn were socially divided into feudal landlords and working farmers. Some of them were well-off villagers, who had lost large portions of their village lands to the government, and who moved to Baba Amr in order to buy a piece from the remainders still in the hands of the ex-feudal owners. They joined the ranks of employers, along with the well-paid managers of the new industrial enterprises on the outskirts of Homs, such as the newly opened petrol refinery and the composting factory. The less well-off villagers were also tempted to leave their traditional life and move closer to the city, starting a new life by purchasing a tenancy in Baba Amr from their fellow liberated farmers.

After the initial expropriations, the government had no particular interest in the area and no intention of upgrading it. Thus, it was left out of the regulatory plan, and title to the land remained floating. Nevertheless, the original clusters of farmers' houses formed a nucleus for proliferation, on which government planners imposed a Cartesian road-map. Baba Amr continued to grow, until its day of doom, as a result of a two-fold internal migration: from the side of the surrounding villages and from the side of the burgeoning city. However, the vast majority of its new inhabitants had something in common: they belonged to those designated in Syria as Turkman – Syrians of Turkish origin, relics of the Ottoman Empire, who had for the most part kept their Turkish traditions and language.

Although Baba Amr grew into a substantial district adjoining the city, with a fluctuating population of almost 25,000, the locality was under-serviced and in a dismal condition from the point of view of buildings and infrastructure. While important public amenities were established in the area – such as a suspended railway, the city's university, a horse-riding club to the south and a public stadium to the north – the value of real estate in Baba Amr itself remained low, and, despite its closeness to the city centre and its enormous potential, it was developed in an entirely random way.

The area sits upon layers of ancient tunnel networks. Remains and relics are buried a few metres underfoot, so that a simple dig might drop you into some previously undiscovered Roman

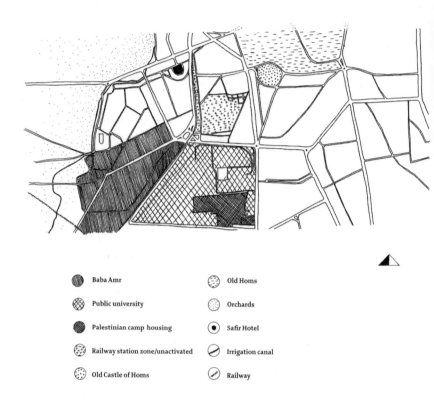

	Baba Amr		Old Homs
	Public university		Orchards
	Palestinian camp housing		Safir Hotel
	Railway station zone/unactivated		Irrigation canal
	Old Castle of Homs		Railway

▲ A general map of Baba Amr (hatched) and its relationship to the city of Homs.

dungeon. Such chance finds had actually occurred before in Baba Amr but were kept secret for fear of property being lost to the governmental department of antiquities.

These hidden cultural treasures were not the locality's only valuable asset. Baba Amr has a unique stretch of fertile land to the west of Homs. This is surrounded first by the city's irrigation canal, and then by the Baba Amr orchards, which have in the past provided 60% of the city's supply of fruit and vegetables. These orchards are located between the canal and the Asi River, in an area of abundant crops.

Since the site is on the edge of and overlooking the Asi River, it was historically maintained as a fortress for the defence of Old Homs. Hence it was called 'the eighth gate', in reference to the original seven gates of the intramural city. Little documentation has survived, so the cultural physiognomy of the locality has to be constructed from eyewitness accounts. These tell of the existence of ancient tunnelling that extends towards the old castle of Homs at the opposite frontier of the city.

From its recent history to its final destruction in 2013 the inhabitants of Baba Amr can be divided into three generations. The first founded Baba Amr as a new part of the city. Its members migrated from the surrounding rural areas to work in the city, producing a second generation who took advantage of the free public education system and also learned to practise a craft. As for the third generation, it was much more distant from country traditions and life-skills and more attracted to the exciting but less spiritually fulfilling life of the modern city.

Turkmans predominated in Baba Amr over the few Kurds and Arabs, but all were Sunni Muslims. They built rustic dwellings on the pattern of village houses: austere single-storey buildings with a usable flat roof and a small courtyard at the rear of the house where a few edible plants and sometimes a tree or two might be grown, depending on the size of the property. These houses were tacked along a Hausmann-style Cartesian plan, with straight streets leading to amorphous squares. As the area continued to grow, each cluster of back-to-back houses had to adapt to the main street network, as laid down by the government. Between the contiguous clusters, people opened their own thoroughfares: narrow winding paths such as a stream might carve into a hillside. Small businesses consisting of tiny shops and grocery stores, along with workshops for clean industries such as carpentry, tailoring and blacksmithing, were dotted in between the dwellings.

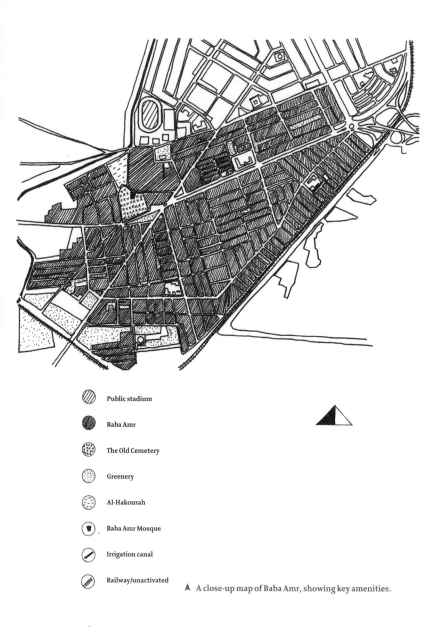

Public stadium	
Baba Amr	
The Old Cemetery	
Greenery	
Al-Hakourah	
Baba Amr Mosque	
Irrigation canal	
Railway/unactivated	

▲ A close-up map of Baba Amr, showing key amenities.

This kind of mixed urbanism, which is a main feature of most Syrian settlements, had no particular order to it. It exhibited neither aesthetic sense nor predetermined design. Despite its spontaneity, the urban growth did not make use of organic local materials or indigenous architectural techniques. Everything was built with monotonous concrete blocks, encasing whatever space was needed.

The resulting clusters were mostly grouped according to family name, forming micro-communities. Each consisted of a single family, although a typical family would have six to ten children and very close ties with an extended family, and consequently with the wider community. The hierarchical social ties resulted in a high sense of security within the entire locality. Children could play freely in the open without immediate adult surveillance, since they were protected by everyone who considered himself to be a 'member' of the locality. The type of security witnessed in Baba Amr did not rely on knowing the other person but on knowing where he was from. With nearly 5,000 residential units over an area of 2.3 square kilometres this was a difficult thing to assure. However, the residents shared a remarkably unified existence, inviting each other as guests, taking care of each other's properties and defending each other's families without hesitation.

This attitude of guardianship, and the community's original attachment to nature, could be detected in urban gestures. For instance, you might find a small pond with raised cement edges created under a tree on the pavement so that birds and cats could drink from it. Or you might find fruitful olive trees lining the streets on the open verges – additions to the otherwise haphazard urban planning process. Such thoughtful details touched my heart when I visited the locality for the first time to meet the parents of my husband, whose path I would never have crossed had it not been for the architecture school, there being little chance for people from different backgrounds to meet and make a life together in our modern divided city.

The marginalization of rural people by urban citizens has deep roots. City people used to threaten naughty children by saying 'a farmer will come and grab you'; and when it came to judging the beauty of a thing, 'rustic' was always a term of abuse. To marry my husband, who was born and raised in Baba Amr, I had to give up the idea of a conventional wedding: our two worlds could not be united even for a night.

I had myself been raised within a family that was highly conscious of class distinctions, and especially condescending towards the 'vulgar' non-city residents. We were separated from those pariahs in our schools, neighbourhoods and streets. It wasn't until college days that I met those 'others' face to face and sat beside them. I remember the first lesson when our professors warned us against such divisions, saying, 'This is an architecture school. Boys will work with girls, and seniors with juniors. Don't sit in groups: mingle and get to know each other, otherwise you won't learn a thing.' They left the implicit meaning unsaid: that the many religions, cultures and social classes that were meeting here for the first time must now work together and learn to move out of the family (the community of destiny) into the profession (a community of choice). I am ashamed to confess my nervous tears at the culture shock of finding so many 'rustic people' at the college. I will never forget how a senior friend tried to put me at my ease, telling me that I should think differently and get rid of such an unhealthy mind-set. He helped me to fit in, although he himself suffered prejudice on account of his rural origins. What the city denied us with its divisive urbanism only the university was at that time able to give back to us.

Later on Syrians were introduced to private schools and private universities that re-enhanced the distinction between social classes and creeds. Indeed, private institutions – banks, colleges, companies – flooded the country throughout the decade before the recent war, changing an economy worn out by corruption into one even more sharpened by polarization. Small businesses and trades came under increasing pressure, and the middle class was burdened more than ever. Predictably, this left its marks on the already damaged social fabric, cutting through the last remaining webs of cohesion. Despite their manifoldness, the old Syrian communities were always homogenous and never heterogeneous, and that was both implied and explicitly expressed in their built environment. The negative changes in the economy, and the moral degeneration that came with uprootedness, meant that the newcomers tended to settle in introverted, semi-isolated groups.

Nevertheless, in the case of Baba Amr, certain additional factors played a part in the formation of unexpected connections with the city. As Turkmans the people of Baba Amr had many valued qualities, including craft skills that required their innate physical strength, in addition to the agricultural experience acquired by owning or working on their previous vast flat lands north of Homs. Craft and agriculture are not to be considered mere means of production that allow people to enter the city on their own terms; they are real-life schooling tools, and bring with them a special sense of decorum that is only understood in their performance. Ask any artisan why he has chosen such a time-consuming profession, and he will struggle to explain the complex relationship between himself and the object on which he works; he will tell you about the 'dialogue' that happens between the two, and the heart and soul that he pours into the result. However, in reality how is such a 'dialogue' conducted, and how can someone pour soul into an object? The same relationship springs up between the farmer and the land: a kind of courtly love that ties him to something that will consume so much of him for the rest of his life, but to which he will always be attached by a vow of fidelity.

The work of the craftsman lifts objects into a world of meaning that we risk losing in our totally mechanized age. 'Marks of human labor' and the 'memorial of an activity' can elicit appreciation even

▲ A craftsman at work.

from those unwilling to acknowledge the value of hand-produced things.[1] But if this goes some way to explaining the appeal of craft production for the consumer, what about the producer? What compels someone to go through such hurdles, to become so 'hooked' on handiwork as to devote his life to it? I believe that the social importance of such a way of production far exceeds its economic benefit, and that its true value is even greater for the producer than it is for the consumer. The value of craft doesn't reside simply in providing essential products for city life; it lies in the way the products are made, and the subliminal education that emanates from them, which is in my view essential for any flourishing society. Such craft production broadens our sense of the universe as an arena for inspiration and creation. Realizing how much it takes to *make* something teaches us the perfection that we can aim for, even if we can never achieve it. Craft products educate us to strive for commitment and allow us to know what it is like to *contribute*. These craft skills, accompanied by formal education (in many cases higher education), empowered the people of Baba Amr to create a self-sustaining community that at a certain point became indispensable to the city. That, in turn, meant encountering city life and urban inhabitants, resulting in a certain level of familiarity and openness.

Baba Amr also established its connection with the city by being the main Syrian home of Sufism. The most influential Sufi figures would gather regularly at the Baba Amr mosque. Well before expansion and urbanization the area had its old mosque, with a graveyard that carried special importance due to the notable Islamic figures buried there. Those Sufi 'masters', many of whom chose to reside in Baba Amr when it was later developed, had a traditional annual festival that was attended by the whole city, and at which a special kind of sweet was made and distributed among the people and their children. This festival would start as a carnival, beginning in the city centre and proceeding towards a vacant hillside in Baba

Amr called Al-Hakourah, where mounted riders performed on horseback and people would assemble to watch. The sweet made at that time of the year was a speciality of Homs and to be found in no other city in Syria. The festivities – combining the social and the religious, the culinary and the sporting, the urban and the rural – had the power to vitalize the whole city, economically and socially. In addition, it engaged people of different urban areas and backgrounds in a single pursuit of pleasure.

Still, the rural traditions of the Baba Amr people and their adherence to their own language prevented them from actually coalescing with the city. Nor were they encouraged to coalesce by the higher social classes there, who continued to look down on them as unwanted 'peasants', and also in some cases as occupiers of their looted property. This unjust stance was adopted widely and for a very long time, even by those who were just as poor as the average Turkman in terms of income. It was also perpetuated by the Turkmans' distinct form of urbanism, limited to one-storey buildings on the rural pattern and kept out of the regulatory plan of the city, to be condemned as 'informal' social housing. Their dwellings also offended against the accepted Homsi lifestyle, with their rustic materials, furniture mostly placed low-level on the floor and the pronounced lack of privacy, social life being practised in the open and with everything on view. As a result, the 'flat system' and its resulting form of settlement was eventually prohibited by the official planners, who, perversely, treated the locality as a kind of leper colony. While regular urban development touched its periphery, it never actually entered. Those people of Baba Amr who contributed to the city as doctors, engineers, professors and athletes, as well as builders, craftsmen and farmers, were marginalized by the built environment as much as they were marginalized by society. With Homs's neat building blocks standing on tip-toe in their backyards, careful not to touch them, they understood the message that they were fated to give to a city that would never give back.

As for the governmental agenda, it obstinately and for no obvious reason maintained the randomness of the area, despite the existence of a regulatory plan. It also prevented the Sufi festival by tacit actions, including erecting two housing blocks on the Hakourah, work on which was interrupted and then resumed over ten years. Later on, those blocks were occupied by families from outside Baba Amr, who kept themselves distant from the life of the locality.

The second generation of Baba Amr, having witnessed the 1980s unrest in which the Muslim Brotherhood were ruthlessly suppressed in Hama, grew up more distant from religious values than the first or the third generations. An atmosphere of mixed fear and perplexity reigned over Syrian communities then. Even if they weren't likely to adopt such deviations from the true spirit of Islam, they still preferred safety over worship. The second generation cohort therefore exhibited a different approach to life matters, including the recent conflict, from the other two generations. The first generation practised its beliefs through a perfect symbiosis with its surroundings, including the built environment (I was astonished to learn that my father-in-law had voluntarily given up nearly a third of his precious property in order to allow a short cut to the neighbouring mosque). The second generation, by contrast, was a vigilant one that had 'the fresh stick's marks on its sides' and waning connections to religious values and identity, though nonetheless the elders were still venerated and deferred to. The majority of the third generation initially grew up to disregard education, craftwork and religious values altogether. Divided into two main cohorts, they shared the same disappointment in what they considered to be the trivial accomplishments of obsolete values. Each adopted a polar opposite of those values in order to set the record straight. The first deviated into extremism and a false conception of religion in order to evacuate its disappointments through hatred. The second chose materialism as a way of life, in order to excuse its pathologies.

What helped even more to create the acid soil in which these kinds of destructive behaviour could germinate was the real estate upturn that occurred in Baba Amr (as in all the informal settlements) in 2009. It was then that tacit approval was granted to those areas to build 'unofficially', in accordance with the long-impeded regulatory plan. This was made possible by pervasive corruption, which spread the word while turning a blind eye to any consequences. Thus, the third generation – distanced from their tradi-

➤ A typical Baba Amr neighbourhood.

tions and rural heritage – started building blocks of up to three storeys, filling every empty square metre with construction, while corrupt officials filled their coffers.

As a result, those coveted modern building types that used to be displayed on Baba Amr's frontier, like freshly baked cakes sitting temptingly behind a counter, were now available to everyone. Building went mad in the area: concrete platforms raised on concrete columns, extending, expanding, layer upon layer and in full

speed before the deal should change. People were buying and selling, stuffing their space with as much building as they could after their previous hand-to-mouth existence. Despite the floating ownership of the land and the illegality of the 'permission', many went overboard, creating a deep sense of profligacy.

After the unrest started, many of the third generation, whether extremist or materialist, were among the first to be tempted to become urban guerillas. Setting aside their contradictory dogmas, they joined forces in order to be in command for a change. They used the roofs of the newly built housing blocks as gun posts to confront the government forces. Inside the area, many guerillas set up their own security checks and seized properties in the name of defiance, adding more pressure to the spartan lives of the innocent residents, who showed remarkable fortitude as their properties crumbled before their eyes.

The governing authorities responded by regarding the fact of coming from Baba Amr as a punishable offence. Antagonism swelled in the countless wounded chests, and a simple statement would be counted as adherence to one or other of the warring factions. The whole area with everyone and everything in it was violently assaulted, and families had to live in the lethal crossfire. The place that they had brought to life was now bringing them death.

In 2011, when all this was just beginning, my husband was preparing to travel to Kuwait to receive an award for his online architecture portal, recognized as the best media project in the Arab world. He had the letter of recognition in his pocket with the plane ticket for five days' time touching his ID, in which was written his birthplace, 'Baba Amr'. An official at an army security checkpoint stopped him and asked for his ID. Then he went missing. I kept dialling his number but the phone was turned off. No one knew where he was. My family and his were searching for him by calling and visiting everyone they knew that had connections with the security services and with prisons. I knew that entering such a place is the equivalent of entering a time machine from which you may never emerge; a black hole into which people can disappear without trace. I couldn't do anything except cry and pray to God that I would see him again.

On the 'other side' he was stripped of his clothes, dragged, handcuffed and tied into a long line of other unfortunates. He was moved from place to place, then stuffed into a suffocating dark room where he could only stand with his face shoved into the back of a fellow prisoner's head. The inmates stood like that for a day, before being moved first thing next morning to another cell, where they were laid down undressed on the filthy floor. My husband is strong and wise, and he chose not to remain silent, nor to allow himself to get frightened. He demanded to see the responsible officer and to be told what his 'crime' was. He used whatever 'cards' he had, which in his case was the letter of recognition. He shouted at the guards, scolding them for not appreciating 'his worth to his country'. He questioned their alleged patriotism for abducting him and standing in the way of such a reward. To his astonishment, his desperate plan worked. He was even able to detect a hint of embarrassment in some of their faces. In the end he was able to persuade the interrogating officer to write down his supposed actual crime, rather than the one that had been stuck to him, which was simply that of being from Baba Amr. To this day, he believes that that piece of paper saved his life.

Back in the cell, he saw a shocking collection of people, and he managed to hear all their stories. They spoke openly to him, because neither his first nor his last name carried any religious connotation, so every group counted him as an honorary member. They talked of their charges and their crimes, and of how much time they had spent in custody. There were people of all creeds, and with all manner of criminal convictions: murderers, drug dealers, robbers, fraudsters, along with political prisoners and warriors from both parties. There were severely wounded, sick and ailing people. All of them were waiting under the yellow light of the cell – which was kept on all the time – to be deported to an unknown fate. After three days and nights, which felt like a lifetime, my husband's whereabouts were luckily determined (which is usually the most difficult part), and he was brought before a judge, who set him free on seeing the preposterous accusation that had been registered against his name. Most people are not so lucky, enduring ordeals without end, and with no re-emergence into the light of day. Many wives and mothers of those taken into the prison cells never dry their tears or hug their loved ones again. My husband considered his experience an enlightening one, from which he emerged with an early revelation to avoid extremism and polarization. He learned, too, that the deeper you sink in society the more crushing the misery you'll find. The millstones are always turning and those caught between them have no escape.

After that time the situation became more and more irretrievable. The chance of smoothing ruffled feathers ceased to exist as the conflict plucked off every plume. In Baba Amr, where heavy military equipment was first used by the government forces, the urban guerillas were admired for their attempt to stand up in the face of the ruthlessly deployed tanks and air force. These, for their part, underestimated a furious resistance that was able to make use of the old tunnel network beneath Baba Amr and to take advantage of the close-knit urbanism. Baba Amr was attacked by tanks and air strikes for months while civilians were still trapped there. The losses were unimaginable for both armies and for those caught in between. High concrete walls were erected to besiege the now-evacuated area, whose people were thereafter either dead, imprisoned or refugees. Those watching from outside were divided, like the cheering crowds at a football match: with the same enthusiasm, the same rage, and as little effect as on the football pitch. As a 'son' of Baba Amr my husband was able to feel this 'heat' in person: a taxi driver might refuse payment for his ride if by chance he learned where my husband was from, while a security guard would flip the ID between his fingers in confusion, concluding, 'I don't know how to deal with you: your ID has one face of hell and the other of paradise', as he compared my husband's birthplace of Baba Amr with his residency of Al-Mahtta, known for its large number of Christian inhabitants.

The government, on the other hand, had a more insidious plan for the defeated locality, confronted by tenacious fighters who were able to conjure themselves between adjacent homes. The locality's urban and demographic physiognomy had to be altered! A new expropriation call was issued for the area, changing shared ownership of the land into complete ownership by the government. Immediately a new regulatory plan was also issued, dividing the area into separate blocks of high-rise towers. The uprooted people of Baba Amr now own nothing; Baba Amr is finished.

To add salt to the wound, completely different measures were taken in other destroyed areas. One could not help but notice the discriminatory approach adopted by officials to the various urban settlements across the country. For instance, the Christian majority town of Ma'aloula near Damascus – the only urban centre in the world that still uses the Aramaic tongue of Jesus Christ – suffered very unfortunate damage to its houses and monasteries carved into the mountainside, but the official approach towards compensating the civilians in this area was radically different from that in places inhabited by the Sunni Muslims. In Christian villages and districts the government removed rubble and provided new infrastructure, whereas for the most part – as if to punish all Sunnis for the anti-government stance of many – Sunni areas have been left without help and their residents have been subject to arbitrary arrest. Thus in the mountain town of Al-Husn, next to Krak des Chevaliers, the Sunni inhabitants were prohibited from returning even to live in the rubble of their homes. When not explicitly prohibited, the return of Sunnis has been met with incapacitating terms and obstacles, if not with mysterious incidents of abduction. People who would have settled for having their windows sealed with cardboard and a scrappy piece of wood placed over the shell holes (for no reconstruction works are allowed in these areas) – people who have lost literally everything, in most cases for committing nothing – have been forced to live the aftermath of destruction with eyes wide open as their 'neighbours' are cosseted and looked after.

Such discrimination vividly recalls the history of the late Ottoman rule in Syria, when corrupt rulers used to pander to foreign interests in order to hold on to a shaky throne, favouring the creeds that the foreigners favoured and condemning the rest. Thus the French preference for the Christian communities in the nineteenth century allowed Christian merchants to control the market in a way that bankrupted many businesses that belonged to Muslims – a fact that caused great resentment, and eventually led to a massacre of Christians in 1860. Ironically, those who saved the situation in the end were not the official government, nor the foreign alliances who stood by watching; it was other Muslims, who, committed to their true religion, stood by their partners in home and life, and protected them inside their own houses despite the cost to themselves.

All of this should also be understood in a modern-day context that combines pervasive officialdom, the degeneration of enlightened moral values, currents of extremism that have used religion as a cover, and of course the divisive urbanism that has zoned communities by religion. In such circumstances, injustice is the match that starts the conflagration. And already we see the foundations being laid for the next bloody conflict. Since the tail-end of Ottoman rule, Syrian society has lived as if on a sine wave, through phases of partial recovery followed immediately by phases of total degeneration. Never yet has it returned to the days of complete health and prosperity that it once enjoyed.

I believe that the disaster of Baba Amr could have been avoided by a fairer form of urbanization. This productive and educated community should have been granted 'payback' through architecture. This was one of the reasons I chose Baba Amr as a case study in my contribution to a UN-Habitat competition. The aim of the contest was to find solutions for revitalizing social and mass housing areas in countries all over the world. I was keen to choose Baba Amr for many reasons, among them its great potential socially, architecturally and economically. In my case, most of my city had been destroyed, so the UN's term 'revitalization' would have to be substituted by 'reconstruction'.

The competition asked (among many other things) for the re-engagement in the production cycle of as many social forces of the community as possible, especially women. Women in Baba Amr were already involved socially and productively, due to the openness of the society. However, their independent efforts had various economic aspects that were not being efficiently exploited. For example, women of all ages in Baba Amr enjoyed productive skills in organic food processing and preserving, considered essential for every home. These processes would usually take place in domestic open-air spaces, namely the roof and the backyard, both of which were indispensable for any family in Baba Amr (most household activities took place there: preparing food, cleaning, gardening, etc.). Thus, not only would the creation of a special courtyard or patio – with added height, space for parking, and landscaped greenery – achieve passive design goals and be convenient for the mainstream lifestyle, but it could also be used to upscale the women's activities and exploit an unused economic asset of the community.

The bicycle – the principal means of transportation in Baba Amr – would have to be taken into consideration as well. A key challenge was to create a road network, bearing in mind the existing routes built upon the city's sewer and power cable network, while maintaining and enhancing the coherence of the urban fabric. This coherence was conditioned by an ability to control the level of openness and privacy permissible, so windows and porches were not to overlook any part of the surrounding inner life of the units. I suggested a 'Tree unit', growing upwards, offering flexibility and the possibility of future vertical growth. The 'trunk' contains mixed-use spaces for shops selling the products of local women and farmers. As the 'Tree' grows, apartments with a private court-yard can branch up in a way that is protected yet still open to the inside and the outside. Each Tree unit holds hands with the surrounding four Trees, composing an urban fabric that is able to grow and spread organically. Underneath the Trees, shaded and open areas are created for parking, gardening, playing and leisure.

The existing Baba Amr had many surrounding amenities that should have been connected to it. It also had many promising

▼ Cross-section of the Tree unit
showing how it is related to the
next unit and how the inner patios
are arranged.

1. Patio

2. Light well

3. Duplex stairs

4. Shops/studios

5. Basement service
(central fuel tanks,
storage...)

6. Potential growth

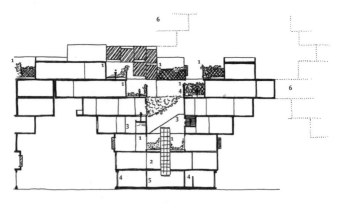

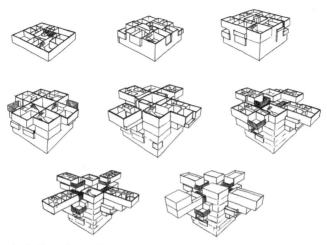

▲ The Tree unit 'growth'.

▼ A street view showing the units 'holding hands', echoing the traditional
   Sibat (a bridge hanging over old alleys resulting from the conjunction of
   two adjacent houses).

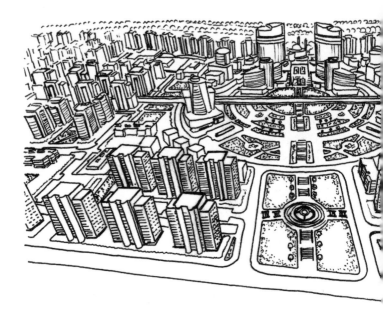

internal activities that could have engaged the locality's potential in the economic cycle of the city. Re-using Al-Hakourah was a main goal of my proposal, too; I didn't want to deny the religious character of the locality, but I wanted to upgrade it and situate it where it might grow in a healthy way, without its residents degenerating into the kind of identity fanaticism that we had already seen. Thus, I suggested that Baba Amr's main mosque should be rebuilt attached to Al-Hakourah, where an urban centre could be created, complete with amenities relating to the people's interests: a park, a library, a display of plants, food carts and open sports spaces, refurbishing Al-Hakourah as a place for all times of the year.

I don't claim that my proposal is the perfect answer to the Baba Amr 'dilemma'; and in any case I worked on it alone, and my resources were limited to a few hours of electricity per day and one set of hands. However, I'm certain that in order to tackle this kind

◄ The official released project for the rebuilding of Baba Amr. Similar approaches are set for all the 'informal' settlements across Syria.

of urban problem we need to start with the social fabric, for that is the ground on which we build. To my great happiness, my competition proposal was recognized and won first place at local level. When it was published online, the reaction was unbelievable. The people of Homs (from their fragmented positions around the world) shared the news on social media, rapidly creating quite a stir. Some thought it was a government proposal, and others believed it was actually going to be commissioned. It was as if no one actually read the content, but only informed themselves by glancing at the headlines and the images. As for the government, it held a few seminars and showcased my proposal (without my knowledge) as one of the options on the table, before checkmating the situation by taking ownership of the land and issuing its own pre-set regulatory plan with free-standing blocks and towers. The most frustrating thing about the whole episode is not that the proposal was undermined by gossip (at one point I was accused of copying from Moshi Safadi's 1970s Habitat), but that the chance of improving a place – based on a better understanding of the inhabitants' psychological and spiritual nature, and expressing all this in a healing form of architecture – was lost forever.

In Baba Amr, those who enjoyed being lifted upon shoulders and greeted as heroes after they were considered pariahs were brutally dropped and left to face their fate. Prejudice among social classes was quickly restored, and with a greater momentum. The losing 'team' of rebels started to receive blame from their former supporters. Covered in blood and despair, they faced resentment to their right and revenge to their left.

It is amazing to me how some humans can be covered in mud and still manage to sniff at others. The few rich who remained living in their districts and didn't move away from all the 'unnecessary noise' had unexpected company to share their buildings and streets: the families uprooted from the informal settlements. These families came to live in the abandoned places, whether schools, unfinished construction sites or private homes which they entered when invited (and sometimes when not invited).

Living among those who had previously been kept apart by urban borders proved to be rather inconvenient for the rich, who continually expressed their resentment at the vulgarity of the newcomers. I can still recall the wincing complaint of a 'friend' about the early morning voices of those who had come to sell their vegetables down the street. After losing their sources of income, some poor residents had come up with an alternative by opening small kiosks of corrugated metal on street corners, even with mortar bombs landing on them every now and then. It was amazing to me that someone would dare to complain of 'noise' while tanks and airplanes were striking just a few hundred metres away. More importantly, how could someone have the audacity to claim social superiority in the face of so much suffering?

This is not just the story of Baba Amr; it is the story of hundreds of settlements that have endured prejudice and injustice, that have been trampled over and over again, until they espoused their own doom. It is the repeated history of the perilous formula of poor planning plus endemic corruption. As for those millions of Syrians who have been trapped between refugee camps and the dismal life of exile or displacement, the question remains: where to go?

5

THE BATTLE FOR A HOME
Nowhere Old, Nowhere New

What is home? The question has haunted me for a long time, and the war in my country has taken me through several stages in search of an answer. At the very moment when I imagine I have arrived at a response, the letters blur before my eyes and become illegible. The truth is that I had no idea what home was before I saw the people of my country killing each other over its definition. But unless they know what 'home' is, architects surely cannot create a settlement or a city.

As a result of my country's war, people have lost both their homes and their cities, sometimes destroying them with their own hands, sometimes watching them disappear beneath the rubble. Some have sold their settlements, others have been sold by them; and this love-hate relationship between people and places has reduced them both to dust. And, as the people are blown hither and thither across the land, the question arises: have they chosen asylum, or been chosen by it? And how long are they going to remain in this state? These questions can be answered with a story – a story that begins with a dream of a home and ends with a dream of Home.

A home of one's own was the eternal dream of every Syrian before the war. You grew up watching people chasing this carrot, with few ever obtaining it. Home-ownership was the ceiling of everyone's aspirations, whoever they were and wherever they came from. The home was not just a place to stay in; it was a guarantee of existence. 'I own a home, therefore I exist.' The first response to any man proposing marriage would be, 'Do you have a home?' and if the answer was yes, then the next question would invariably be 'Own or rent?' And then everything was clear, since the chance of owning a home, unless by inheritance or theft, was roughly equal to the chance of becoming president.

A doctor or an engineer would flog himself, not to achieve a major breakthrough or invent a revolutionary device, but to collect the price of his dream home before death collected him. But why has this dream been so difficult to achieve? Syria is not Japan, in terms of space per capita. It is a sequence of vertical ecological regions, from the Mediterranean shore where a few linear cities are squeezed between adjacent lush mountains with their scattered towns and villages, through the green basin areas where most of the cities are, to the vast arid interior where there is little development. There is plenty of space, and the weather is not bad. The four seasons are distinct and equal, as in a science lesson. Over 34% of the population are of young working age. And yet none of these productive forces can fulfil humanity's basic requirement, which is shelter.

Following the expropriations of the 1950s, the government adopted five-year plans and legislation designed to turn the population towards an industrial economy. To this end it gathered up people from towns and villages and brought them to places of production. In 1953, municipalities were assigned the task of creating social housing to accommodate the newcomers. In 1961, the General Housing Organization was created in order to study the situation and implement the necessary policies. The housing hydra then began to grow its many heads: the Ministry of Housing and Construction, the General Organization for Housing, the Regional Planning Committees, the Ministry of Local Administration, and the General Authority for Real Estate Development and Investment. This monster has snapped at the hopes of Syrians through 11 five-year plans, so that in 2010 unmet demand stood at 1.5 million units, while 40% of all housing was of the 'informal' kind – in other words improvised and without proper incorporation into any urban plan. According to the 2010 census, the urban population formed 56% of the total: of these, 9 million – in other words, nearly 50% of the total population – were living in slums and informal housing. Despite this, 23% of housing units were registered as vacant.

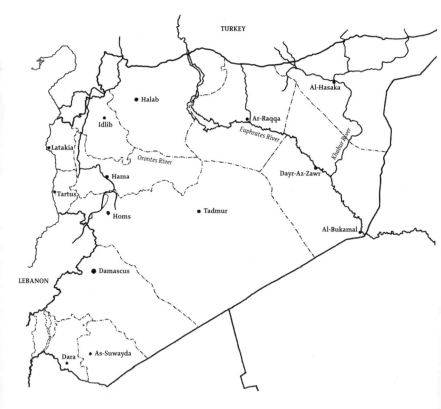

▲ A general map of Syria, showing the provinces' administrative zones, main rivers and main cities.

Why this failure to meet the demand for housing? It cannot be because there is not enough land: how else could the informal housing complexes have been built? Nor is the construction industry failing: the new buildings filling entire districts around the cities are proof of its strength. The relevant factors are, rather, these: the quality of the new housing, the infrastructure, location and demography of the districts where it is being built, and of course most importantly the cost of the buildings themselves. For the whole process of locating, planning and building is entirely corrupt and in the hands of what is publicly called the 'real estate mafia'.

Clusters of raw buildings pop up in remote and isolated locations, with absolutely no urban or architectural planning: free-standing concrete blocks of awkward configuration and meaningless internal arrangement. Every detail of these projects speaks of inhumanity: shape, size, organization of rooms – all is as though wilfully done against nature. After approaching the block across bumpy ground littered with construction cast-offs, your shoes covered in dust, you have to choose between a rail-less stairway and a wobbly elevator (should the lift-well actually be filled with one; this is a rare luxury), in order to reach the dream home for which you have waited twenty years and tightened your belt until you have a Barbie-doll waist. All the surface finishes are shabby and as though glued on, waiting to fall off at the first slam of a door. The ceilings are low and oppressive, the rooms arranged without logic or order, the doors too narrow for furniture to pass through, and the windows badly fitted so that breezes whip your neck wherever you sit.

You try to find a single clean edge in your brand-new nest but you fail. Wherever the walls meet the floor or the window frames are cut into the walls there are smudges of paint and plaster, slapped over the uneven joins. You try to get over the 'aesthetic' aspect and focus instead on the positive fact that you have finally broken free from skyrocketing rent fees at the end of every month and from the nomadic life, constantly packing up and moving while playing the ruthless game of real-estate dealing. You try to remember how long you have waited to have a place of your own where you don't have to live in one room at your parents' or in-laws'. But the roaring sound coming from the water tap you turned on to wash your face is a wake-up call, slapping you on that very face, because there is no water; the non-existent infrastructure of the place means that you have to purchase your own water by begging a wandering container driver to come to your remote area.

You have escaped the rental market only to be at the mercy of the service market. You will have to be constantly occupied from now on in obtaining water, electricity, drainage and other life essentials. The rest of your life will be spent propping up your dream home, which in the end has far more need of you than you of it.

How were these Frankenstein housing projects created? Under the five-year housing plans the government formed partnerships between the public, private and cooperative sectors to sell pieces of

▼ Sub-standard 'dream homes': remote, unfinished, modern social housing tower blocks built by the government.

land to contractors, requiring no vision or planning strategy, and with intrusive corruption all along the way. The lure was the availability of public loans offered by the land bank and similar public institutions, which encouraged people to register for their dream home, paying in advance and condemned to spend the rest of their productive life enslaved to the debt.

In 2002, the General Housing Organization launched the largest program of Housing for the Young, declaring that the government would finance 30% of it without interest. This was to be followed by other projects, such as Housing for Workers, Savings Housing and Popular Housing. Nevertheless, the dismal situation remained unchanged, while fraud and corruption scandals proliferated. The cities extended octopus-like arms studded with stalled construction works and ugly vacant blocks, next to the burgeoning 'informal' housing and slums. Meanwhile the government issued yet more legislation, adding corrective laws to the previous failing ones. The hydra grew a few more heads, with more committees and experts. Foreign planners were called in, through the EU, to draw up plans and prepare studies that would never leave the table. Moving blindly with no urban vision, the government finally announced the Supreme Committee of the National Housing Strategy in 2004, to work on developing an official Housing Policy. Needless to say, the strategy did not see the light of day. People continued to build the unplanned 'informalities', taking responsibility for themselves and enduring all the growing problems of infrastructure, services and sanitation, while real estate in the cities became the most lucrative kind of business and for most people beyond the reach even of a dream.

In such a market an architect is a ghost architect. He has no role in creating visions or suggesting improvements; if lucky, he will be called in by some well-off family to refurbish their interior, according to a standardized taste. Those who manage to climb high enough to take part in the EU legation's planning consultation or similar collaborations with foreign or public bodies will most likely have had to pass through the prescribed network of sycophancy and corruption. The architect's mission in such circumstances is a long way from creating places that will nurture us with peace and beauty, suggesting moral sentiment and lasting values, and defining for us a greater sense of Home.[1]

How can an architect create Home in any building when he himself has never experienced it; when all that he has seen around him is a trampled life that seeks relentlessly to emerge, like the persistent green shoots that spring up from the smallest cracks in the tarmac of a road? Home is the goal of architecture, and a true home is like a mirror that always shows us our best profile, no matter where we stand in relation to it. But when a building shows only our worst side, and when it is the wreckage of our dreams, then it is no longer a home, and nor is it architecture.

The quest for home in Syria has become a rat-race with the government; a constant plotting to find some way to extend a metre or two sideways into a porch, or upwards onto a roof. As if on standby, most new constructions are incomplete, awaiting the next stage of legislation. Then every now and again the government reverts to its favourite game and orders demolition instead.

This kind of built environment sends a clear message of atrophy, and of the subversion of moral and social values. It is visible in the aesthetic devastation: a jungle of misshapen and inhuman forms, in which survival is not just for the fittest, but for the wildest and the greediest. In short, it is tangible as a precursor to war. And of course that is what we have witnessed, as human beings were wiped out, together with their shadows, which were their homes. These shadows were hit, punctured and tortured like the bodies that produced them, and now they lie in ruins.

Millions of people are now displaced and uprooted, wondering, in their changed life that can only get worse, where to go, what to hold on to, where to cut losses and where to take risks. Some have had the luxury of reflecting on these questions for a while; others have had to make a decision while covered in blood and fleeing under fire. Disasters, both natural and man-made, are habitual occurrences on earth, but when you lose your home, and the land that your home once sat upon, and when you lose them in a world that has not decided to which party you have lost them, and when you lose them without ever knowing when and from whom they might be regained, if ever, that's when you have lost your shadow in this world, the proof of your being here, under the shared light of the sun.

Not all who have left their homes were absolutely compelled to do so; some have chosen to leave, in various different ways. Some were wealthy enough not to have to persevere or have patience; they found no reason to stay when there was a clear alternative. They were able to buy their tickets out and resume their lives in countries such as the Lebanon, UAE, Egypt and Turkey, or in the USA or Europe. Many such people haven't lost their homes in any case, since they were located outside the eye of destruction. If these people could have persevered, life in their urban areas would have been difficult but not impossible.

Others enjoyed the luxury of choice without having the money to buy security at the end of it. These citizens were tempted by the seemingly half-open door of the Western world, which they had always considered the gateway to prosperity. The coveted grass on the other side, which has always promised advancement and order, is now only a boat ride away. Naturally, war merchants have not left this lucrative niche market untapped: organized networks of human trafficking have stretched their strings across all borders, while people have encouraged one another to leave the mess behind and trust in the promised heaven that is Europe.

Those people who sell all they have, and launch themselves towards a rumoured prosperity overseas, explain their choice by reference to the future death of their country, which they them-selves, out of covetousness, have sentenced to death. By contrast, those who stay to endure the bombs and the bullets have clung to what matters to them most, which is the network of attachments and responsibilities that has grown here, in what was once their home. Of course these attachments, too, are jeopardized, so there are other reasons to migrate besides the loss of one's home or livelihood: having a young son, who might at any time be drafted into the army or kidnapped for ransom or thrown into prison (a highly lucrative business has evolved between officers, attorneys and judges), has become an urgent reason for many to leave.

Home has also taken on another definition for many of the uprooted: not a place of temporary shelter, grudgingly accepted for a few days or months, as in the aftermath of some natural disaster, but a sanctuary that has been lived in for years already, and from which there is no foreseeable exit, despite intolerable conditions. People in the country areas around the northern city of Idlib have been forced to live in orchards, or even caves, caught in the crossfire between the battling war fronts – sometimes hit by the official army, sometimes by the alliance opposing them; unable to escape and without electricity, running water, doctors or any of the conveniences of modern life. Only women can go out in search of provisions, since men would be instantly arrested. Food comes from the farmland, any excess being traded with the besieging troops. Every sunrise brings a major shift in events. As I write, Idlib has fallen to the opposition, which means more dramatic changes, new forms of homelessness, new forms of torture for the local people who pay the price for every victory, no matter whose it is.

Internal displacement usually takes the form of people being forced from their homes into temporary shelters ('temporary' here being a euphemism). The shelters mostly consist of buildings belonging to state schools. These schools have a single unified design, reminiscent of a prison: an L-shaped block covered by sprayed beige stucco, on whose spiky surface you have to be careful not to scratch yourself. The windows are covered with a fine metal mesh that holds the sky at bay. As children we used to stand by the mesh, pushing our little fingers through the holes, like convicts behind bars. Today these sheets support pouches that hang from them on wires: the closets and cupboards of the people who sleep on the sponge mattresses spread beneath them. Their bathrooms are the communal toilets, with one deep wall-long trough that we, as children, were so repelled by that we would contain ourselves all day until we got home, rather than make use of them. Families – the very old and the very young included – make their homes here, the borders of which are defined by a single bed-sheet pinned to the ceiling.

▼ One type of temporary shelter: pre-fabricated caravans placed on the playground of an evacuated school.

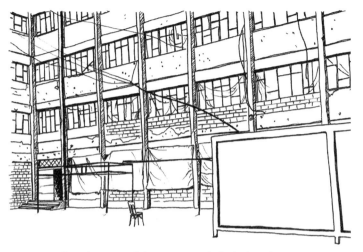

▲ A second form of temporary shelter: an evacuated school, whose classrooms will be used as 'homes'.

Alternatively, displaced people are stuffed into the unfinished concrete blocks, seized in the course of the war, and eloquent expressions of the brutality all around, with their bare concrete surfaces, exposed cables (if there is any power at all) and sheets of cardboard for window shields.

Or there is the best case scenario: obtaining the home of someone who is leaving, who might give you the deeds out of charity, by way of lending out the place for a while, or by way of a cooperative agreement in which you undertake to protect the home from vandalism while the owner is away. Of course all such agreements become provisional as the chaos worsens.

The government that crippled our civil society in order to maximize its own control has effectively precluded sympathy between the settled community and the displaced. Shockingly, philanthropic people who have donated food or money to the new 'school residents' have sometimes been arrested, since officially these needy people were only allowed to receive help from international organizations, under strict political terms. In Syrian streets today you can see 'homes' carried along in a plastic bag or on a bicycle. Many children who open their eyes on this world have not known what it is to belong to a place that belongs to you. Young children of eight or nine go out to grab the 70 cm-wide mattresses that are sometimes distributed as humanitarian aid, and get back 'home' thrilled with this new 'room' of their own. For years now the public parks of Damascus have been 'homes' for the homeless, but nowadays even the settled have become homeless and have found themselves living in the rubble of half-demolished rooms under ceilings that might fall at any time. Of course, there are sad stories of the homeless to be told of every major city, but the catastrophe of the homeless in this war does not reside only in the swarms of displaced people, but in the social fissures that have resulted. A new generation is being born and raised without true belonging, without a shared identity, and without education or values, knowing only that there is no place in this world to call their own.[2]

In Syria people haven't just lost a part of their identity; they have lost most of their built history and all of their present. They are living in fragmented ruins, with only a hazy memory of their identity as citizens of a shared territory and home. Identity in all its forms depends on continuity and memory, and architecture is the main publicly recognizable register of that. Of course architecture is not the axis around which all human life rotates, but it is our most effective register: a dynamic and interactive one that has the power to suggest and even direct human activity. In that sense, settlement, identity and social integration are both the producers and the product of effective urbanism. Registered continuity and collective memory are most visible through architecture, which marks out a place as 'ours'. Take away such signs and symbols of citizenship and the result is a war of 'identities' in the other sense: factitious groupings identifying with each other on the basis of a misreading of religion and a desperate need to define 'us' against 'them' – to define identity not by what we all share but by what excludes others.

Identity in the positive sense stems from the power of *accomplishment*, which I suggest is the key measure of acceptance among disparate social groups and communities. The way this accomplishment is weighed is affected by the media, but the kind of accomplishment I have in mind is that which belongs to civilization and can be a source of national pride. Old monuments and artefacts are part of such an accomplishment, and contribute to our sense of who we are. Two types of accomplishment shape people's sense of identity: those that give them pleasure (either through beauty or some other value), and those that make them proud (through continuity and a sense of contribution). Both are made tangible in the built environment, through those details that call to us with the voice of home: the beauty of a window frame or a decorative moulding, the shade of a planted tree, memories from childhood of the door through which one entered into safety and love, reminiscences from later years of the atmospheric background to friendships and family ties. The pleasurable experience of place through its configuration is part of what attaches us to it – part of what makes it into a 'there', a durable and recognizable frame within which our individual lives occur, and one which helps to make us a part of one another. Values are implied and sustained by this kind of configuration, helping to attach people in another way to what is deep in themselves and what demands a shared and civilized identity.

If a place offers architectural details that give pleasure to the eye, as well as moral values implicit in their creation, order and configuration, then the inhabitant will experience joy and consider that place to be *their accomplishment*; their identity.[3] Likewise, places that have had the power to survive through many generations or civilizations can be considered an accomplishment by every inhabitant. People can see themselves in relics and ancient ruins because they imagine the victory of their ancestors (even if it was only the victory of surviving) as a victory for themselves. They also see these things as a validation of their present existence. The pride that accompanies such accomplishments unites the collective self and creates an identity based on the sharing of a place, a 'there' to which they belong. If people weren't able to find traces of these accomplishments, whether through pleasure or pride, they would have no sense of belonging and would look for their identity elsewhere, perhaps in those factitious antagonisms that put a crossfire of hatred where once there was a shared street.

This raises the question of accomplishment in relation to the social acceptance of disparate groups. I believe that people unconsciously weigh the 'other' on the scale of accomplishment. Imagine finding a special shop counter set up for shoppers coming from different countries. How would the varying products on the counter be judged? Surely they would be judged in terms of social stereotypes. The observer would evaluate the nature and worth of the products in terms of his knowledge of the accomplishments of the country for whose citizens they were reserved. His stereotyping would of course be much influenced by the media. If the shoppers at the special counter were Japanese, known for their innovative technology and the precision of their workmanship, this might draw other people to that counter, too. If, however, the shoppers were from a different country known, say, for its manufacture of ersatz products, then the appeal of the counter would be diminished, since fake accomplishment is not a kind of accomplishment, but the opposite.

The same kind of reasoning operates when people try to negotiate acceptance and non-acceptance among separate groups. Thus, before the war, well-off Syrians had acquired the habit of hiring a home help from a South East Asian country, such as the Philippines or Indonesia. These women were treated (in most cases) like slaves; their human rights were flagrantly violated until war came to abolish them altogether. They were not allowed to be seen in the presence of their employers, even though they were responsible for looking after their children. But the same employers would be more than happy to be around other foreign nationals such as Europeans, since this was an index of their sophistication. This kind of unethical stereotyping depends very much on an unconscious idea of civil accomplishment.

The same idea influences decisions on whether to accept or reject new settlements. After the Lebanese government issued the statement that it would not accept any more Syrian refugees, an exception was made for the Assyrians who were being oppressed by ISIS in northern Syria and Iraq. Clearly, political factors and genuine duties of care are involved here, but nevertheless one cannot deny the associations attached to this social group, which to this day carries the name of a once great civilization known for its lasting monuments. A significant part of the reactions towards the Syrian refugees' new settlements all around the region can be understood in this way. In Egypt, for example, Syrians have been greeted and welcomed, being known in Egypt for their life skills and for the adaptation skills that have enabled them to excel in several occupations at once. By contrast, the Lebanese judge themselves to be superior for being closer to Western culture, and they therefore deem Syrian accomplishments to be vulgar. In Jordan, Syrians are considered bitter rivals. In Turkey, the old Ottoman attitudes persist in the form of chauvinism, which regards all subject peoples of the Sultanate as inferior.

Of course identity threat is also a key factor in the reception of refugees. A country such as Egypt has a population total that vastly outnumbers that of Syria, and therefore the arrival of even a few hundred thousand Syrian immigrants poses no long-term threat to Egyptian national identity. When coexistence is secure, the measure of accomplishment can be safely applied.

On the part of the refugees, we hear cries for help that after a while turn into cries of frustration. 'Where is humanity?', 'Why don't people sympathize?' Why are such questions important for us to understand settlement? The answer to *why* we sympathize is inherent in *how* we sympathize. And this is crucial to settlement because in the end settlement means acceptance and integration.

Drawing on the psychology of Jean Piaget, Lawrence Kohlberg presented his theory of the various stages of moral development, in which he revisited arguments that had occupied Muslim scholars at the tail end of the thirteenth century. The discussion among those scholars originally concerned the question of whether goodness and a sense of right and wrong are inherent to rational beings. They illustrated the question with the example of a drowning person, and this example is as important for us, in considering the question of moral sympathy, as it was for those early scholars.

Imagine a drowning person in a river, crying out for help, and the different moral premises from which the person watching might decide to act. The scholars' discussion summarized four different premises. First, what Kohlberg was to label 'self-interest driven behaviour' – that of the person who decides to save the other, for example, because he is rich and likely to give his rescuer a generous reward. The second case is that in which the rescuer decides to help through a sense of what is socially acceptable. For example, he may think there is somebody watching, or he may reflect on the consequences to his reputation were the drowning person after all to save himself. Kohlberg identified this type of person as exhibiting conventionality and conformity. In the third case, the rescuer pictures himself in the other's situation. Kohlberg calls this 'reversibility' or, colloquially, 'moral musical chairs'. Muslim scholars called it 'supposing the reverse' (*saba al-tasawar ila al-aks*) and it is what we refer to today as 'humanity', in which our sympathy for the other is essentially a sympathy for ourselves. The final case, for the scholars, was what Kohlberg called 'transcendental morality', in which religion is the basis for moral thinking. Kohlberg ranked these types of reasoning (and added more) hierarchically. However, the scholars did not divide them thus; they saw them as part of a dynamic process.

Such discussions help us to understand how empathy, extended to the victims of a crisis, can turn to its opposite over time. People without the transcendental morality provided by religious belief, those who depend on sympathy alone for moral guidance, can soon be overcome by self-interest and cease to 'suppose the reverse' in their moral dilemmas. We should not blame such people for their inhumanity, but instead recognize the frailty and transience of everything human.

In any case, we cannot be surprised that so many Syrians who left their country willingly have returned back home, despite all the inconvenience, having failed to belong. Those places commonly referred to in Arabic as 'alien countries' can truly be alienating for a native Syrian, and anything but a 'home'. The feeling of alienation is often exaggerated by factors such as language and religion, or food and weather. In all cases alienation comes about when people realize that they have no 'back' to lean on, no collective accomplishment that will enhance their standing in a place of strangers.[4] In the modern world, the absence of such accomplishments – which are often found displayed and endorsed in the built environment – cannot be compensated for either by money or by individual achievements.

Consider the life of the nomad, who has no attachment to built forms. Belonging, for a nomad, is never to a place; his reference points are derived from his tribe. He has no 'home', and no accomplishment apart from his lineage and the proof that it has survived through time. We see this kind of identity expressed in many passages of the Bible, in which a person's title to our consideration is earned by a long genealogy, telling us that A begat B, who begat C, who begat D, down to the point where the narrative begins.

This lack of belonging to a place is something that modern societies have tried to overcome, since tribalism has perilous social consequences. Wise urbanism, especially in a country like Syria, must set out to overcome the pathologies that arise from tribal ways of thinking, and to generate in their stead a sense of belonging to a place, and being part of the community that has made its home there. To do this our architecture must pay due attention to the sense of beauty, and the social significance of built forms, as well as manifesting a healthy 'national pride'. We should not be building our cities as though they were the temporary shacks of nomads.

Of course, the situation in Europe is in no way comparable to that in Syria and elsewhere in the Middle East. Nonetheless the so-called 'advanced countries' are also struggling with problems due to mass immigration and the need to adapt to pressures that the infrastructure was not built to accommodate. I read about the heterogeneous urbanism, involving zoning by race and religion, in the northern British cities, and in Paris and other major French conurbations, and I recognize the beginnings of the kind of instability we have witnessed so disastrously here in Syria. We might think we are different from each other, but the truth is that we are all human. Does it then follow that the European aversion to receiving more immigrants has no justification? If it is an expression of tribalism, then, yes, we need to be wary. But if it is in defence of a long-fought-for sense of accomplishment then no one should argue with it.

Whether we like it or not, a significant number of immigrants are leaving behind places that have struggled with their accomplishments, and have no clear 'point of departure' from which its citizens can orient themselves in the world. It is just such immigrants who are most likely to suffer from abuse and prejudice – not simply because they are different but because they no longer have a 'back' to lean on. They are consequently much more likely to settle in marginal zones of cities, to live in cliques and thus prompt the wider society to increase their sense of isolation.

Without the collective accomplishment that would support them and invite respect from the world and from themselves, they will always be the underdog trying to find a 'home'. And, if they cannot return home quickly, what of their children? The next generation would have to move towards a psychic state that has the relevant departure points. Will this new generation be able to dissolve into the new society, or will it always struggle for an accomplishment of its own? How long might that take? Would it happen as a smooth metabolic process, or would it be more like a chemical reaction with the experiment exploding at the slightest miscalculation?

Although so many people were compelled – in every sense of the word – to leave their homes in Syria, there were a considerable number who chose to migrate to 'gleaming' Europe, dreaming of a ready-made future there, only to be culturally shocked because they had been accustomed to receiving much more for much less effort. They remembered the generosity of their motherland. In Syria, you can literally throw a seed in the soil, forget about it and come back to find a sapling. Food is available the whole year round: every month – not just every season – an entirely new array of food grows out of the ground. Its people have also accumulated expertise over the centuries on the Silk Road, compiling an invaluable repository of social understanding and practical experiences, in addition to the knowledge of craftsmanship, building, industry and trade, not to mention a wealth of cultural treasures and natural resources.

It would be naïve to expect that those who have built their accomplishment with sweat and blood will share it easily with someone who is used to 'being spoiled by his mother'. Of course I'm not saying that less 'sweat and blood' has been shed in my country (it is sadly right now swimming in pools of it), but the truth is that Syria is a country with enormous human and natural capital, and that makes it relatively easy to accomplish things there, and so it has been targeted by considerable foreign greed. Yes, this country has been misused and misled, and, yes, countless people have been gratuitously wronged. But people don't lose their homes, their cities, their accomplishments and their identity, as we have done, without themselves being in great part to blame for it. We didn't lose all that in the final collapse that was aired on national TV screens around the world. No, we have been losing it bit by bit long before that.

In Syria we have an aphorism: 'One who has no old has no new.' I used to look at this as a nostalgic way of attaching oneself to out-moded traditions. Today I think I know better. Since we lost our 'points of departure', we have no longer been able to 'orient our-selves towards the world'. All our accomplishments have been erased, starting with the built ones and ending with the living ones. Our tenets have been shaken and our ground has been destabilized, so no matter how many homes those displaced Syrians try to build outside their country they won't be able to integrate or feel less alienated. Because they have lost their back, their home and their identity. Prior to this war, many brilliant young Syrians used to feel obliged to leave a country that oppressed their talents and ambi-tions through corruption and neglect, but still they struggled day and night to be successful wherever they were so as to buy a home back in Syria. Although they might not visit for years, they couldn't accept the idea of being 'uprooted'. Less fortunate young people, meanwhile, remained trapped, scratching the high walls with their fingers in order to climb up and maybe have a home before the end of their lives. All were trying to hold on to a piece of an accomplish-ment, to grasp even an unravelling thread of their precarious iden-tity, until it all collapsed.

One can only wonder why this identity crisis was so prevalent. And one can only ask: how is our identity to be rebuilt after such massive destruction? On what ground was it standing, and can it be re-established there? And the most important question for this book: what role has architecture to play in all this?

6

THE BATTLE FOR CONTINUITY
Building on the Past for the Future

'Kids, put your clothes on!' – my words after hanging up from
a conversation with my PhD professor on 24 July 2014 at 13:35.

It was a hot summer's day, the city was suffering from recurrent
blackouts that continued for hours and sometimes for days, the
mortar missile phase was still on, and it was the last day of Ramadan
(the fasting month when we refrain from eating and drinking from
dawn until sunset) before the holiday of Eid. My professor and I
had been battling against all odds for me to obtain a doctorate in
architecture. On that unforgettable day things reached a peak.
Certain members of the educational staff at the university had
explicitly declared war on us: they had refused to set a date for the
defence of my thesis and on that day my professor, after countless
attempts to get the date set, was challenged by them to do the
impossible – to get three posters printed, announcing the defence,
before the end of office hours at 14:15.

'Marwa, can you do it?' asked my professor on the phone. I replied,
'I have to, don't I?' I couldn't leave my children unattended and my
husband was at the other end of the city. There was no electricity
and only one remaining stationery shop with its own power generator, and that was almost 800 metres away. I had to go there on
foot, with the children, because at that time no cab could be trusted
not to abduct you, and it was in fact faster on foot because of security checkpoints and roadblocks. So we ran and ran, and by the time

we reached the printing centre my husband was already waiting for us and my little son was exhausted. I printed out the posters and set off for the university with my husband's instructions ringing in my ears: no cabs, no running at the sight of security checks (because you might get shot), and no travelling without my daughter to minimize the chances of being apprehended.

The two of us ran uphill along the empty road, under the close overhead sun, passing the sand bags and fortified buildings occupied by official forces, while every now and then a car with black tinted glass would pass us by, making my heart sink. We climbed over the bridge that overlooks the demolished Baba Amr to the right, heading down towards the university. I was very thirsty and very afraid for our lives, but I was determined to win the challenge and to beat those who had been fighting me gratuitously for years.

We slowed down in front of the checkpoints but not to the degree of being willing to stop. My professor and my husband were alternately checking on us by phone. We reached the doors of the architecture faculty by 14:18: my professor had managed to hold the dean and others until that time. On seeing my red sweaty face his look was both glad and sad. He was thrilled that I had managed to make it, and he was upset because of all the trouble that we had being going through for months. Our opponents were shocked and confused, knowing that when those posters were put up around the faculty they would not be able to go back and the defence would have to be held, whether they liked it or not. They even tried to make silly excuses, such as 'There's no tape to stick the posters up.' They were very taken aback that I had the posters with me.

According to the faculty's rules, the announcement had to be posted on the department walls a few days before the defence, and at that time of year it meant I only had that one day before the holiday of Eid. Otherwise the stalling game that they had been playing for over eight months would continue, with absurd new excuses week by week, holiday by holiday, and meeting by meeting. The ringleader in all this was the head of the design department. This largely unqualified professor had reached his position – as had most of his colleagues – because of the war, which had killed three of the faculty's best members and displaced many others. The arena was thus left empty for the impostors to wet the mud even more.

Before leaving for the holiday this man walked past me and my daughter posting the announcements, entered the dean's office to place a piece of paper face down on the desk, then strutted out. Only my professor and the dean were left in the whole university. As my daughter and I rested on the ground (there were no benches for waiting), I heard the voices getting louder from the dean's office and I knew that something was wrong. I intuited that this tiring journey wasn't meant to reach its end here. Both of them came out and I could see the disappointment and embarrassment on my professor's face. They told me that I had to take the announcements down and go home.

I simply said 'OK' and took the posters down. Later my professor drove me home in his car and explained what was on the piece of paper. Apparently the head of design had been able to claim that he'd had no time to read the dissertation, even after having more than the legal time of three months. My heart was full of disappointment, as was that of my professor. The situation was totally unfair. The importance of the little word 'why' is a topic to which I will return in the context of judging architecture, but in the case of the incomprehensively aggressive treatment of my dissertation the answer seemed to be: 'because they can'.

This was not the beginning of their malice, and it certainly was not the end, and it was expressed against any student who tried to defy their unjust authority. But after that day things heated up into open war – the war of suppression that has been forced upon thousands of young people like me trying to do something with their lives. Official corruption is no secret in my country, nor is the extraordinary policy of finding the exact opposite of the right person for a job in so many fields (the policy of 'negative selection', or 'the survival of the unfittest', much commented upon by the observers of Communist systems). But the most frustrating thing is that those who came to believe they had the powers of gods seemed to seek not only to snuff out the dreams and hopes of so many talented people but also to snuff out whatever hopes they might have had for themselves. Their behaviour was the cause of the brain drain that had afflicted our country long before the war and that made their own careers in the end all but meaningless.

The idea for my research had germinated when I was watching on TV the early demonstrations in Egypt against the Mubarak regime. I remember clearly the image of a line of security guards clashing with the swarms of people flooding Tahrir Square. I was watching the angry faces of the crowds against the black helmets of the guards. Then it occurred to me: what if the guard wasn't wearing his bullet-proof black uniform? What would he look like then? Would that man be looking at him with the same anger and frustration? Who was that guard anyway? Was he convinced by what he was doing? Then, in a Eureka moment, I turned to my husband and told him I knew what I wanted to focus on in my research. I wanted to study the way in which people react towards Islamic architecture as those Egyptians reacted towards that guard! They didn't think of him as a person; they saw him as a representative of a fixed idea, with which he may or may not in fact be identifiable. If the uniform was not there, everything would be different. Regardless of the cause, the collective action was motivated automatically by the appearance of the guards.

Of course, I wasn't discussing the validity or otherwise of the political act; I was focusing my thinking on that particular heated moment. I hadn't yet taken notice of 'stereotyping' as a term, or read about it –

not until after I presented the concept to my professor and then started to 'dig'. What has concerned me the most since my Master's is the quest for 'identity' that has dominated architectural research in my country, both academically and practically. Most of the region's architectural discourse has been preoccupied by this quest. It caught my attention while studying that we don't have a serious architectural form of critique or theorizing; most of our discussions have simply been about the search for that wretched lost identity! Terms such as 'originality', 'locality', 'globalism', 'Arabic architecture' vs. 'Western architecture' dominate the literature, conferences and academia. But this has led to no conclusions and has accomplished nothing other than either celebrating an adulated 'past' or despising it in order to glorify the modernized West. Furthermore it was precisely this narrow-minded obsession with identity that had erupted in the violence that was destroying our country.

When I was a senior student, my graduation project was a World Trade centre in Damascus. My design received almost the lowest grade in the class (this, unfortunately, counted for 40% of the sum of all grades in five years of study) because one professor thought that such a project should have been designed in the 'Arabic style'. This was my awakening. Since that day I have wanted to know what this 'Arabic style' might be. Why is it defined by certain elements of patio, arcades, vaults and geometric patterns? Hence I chose academic research in order to refute what I thought was the kind of pseudo-architecture that I was being taught to emulate.

Our identity crisis was the main leitmotif of the entire architectural scene in the Arabic region. Clearly we seemed not to be able to produce a style of our own without paying tribute to the Islamic tradition. But this tradition in turn was the subject of highly polemical arguments. I set out to show that these arguments had overlooked imperative aspects of their subject. Islamic architecture has stimulated the curiosity of scholars, historians and architectural critics, both regionally and in the West. They have (especially the

Westerners) presented very informative works documenting, analysing and categorizing what has remained of this architectural tradition, disputing how to study and evaluate it, and how even to give it a name. However, it seemed to me through my research that most of those works had something in common that their authors had overlooked: discussion of the *architectural experience*.

The centrality of experience seemed to have been lost between two scholarly fantasies. On the one hand there was that of the Orientalists, who tended to view Islamic architecture as mere decorated surfaces associated with the desert and nomadism (architecture as a temporary relief from carpets, so to speak), even though much of it was accomplished in flourishing urban centres. On the other hand there was the fantasy of Sufism, which has gone overboard in its search for poetic and symbolic messages without any supporting grounds in the physical reality.

In the Arabic-speaking regions, researchers have tended to focus on passive design issues and local construction techniques, treating certain architectural elements with a 'copy-paste' approach and hoping that way to 'generate identity'. I was curious about this collective approach towards 'generating identity'. It didn't make sense to me to use disjointed elements of physical forms – a dome here, a patio there – in order to attain a result that could be described in retrospect, but never prescribed in advance. It was as though Borromini had set out to build 'baroque' churches, two hundred years before Wittkower had invented the term.

Examining the Arabic regions' architectural language, the mainstream prescription for identity in the modern age has been 'to be original and contemporary'. By this is meant combining certain 'authentic' elements with modern design approaches that have no relation to the practices and principles that created the original elements. From my perspective the terms 'original and contemporary' carried an ontological contradiction from the beginning: what is 'original' and not 'contemporary', or 'contemporary' and not 'original'? And why do we need either of those phenomena if it does not have the other contained within it?

The application is questionable, too, because it takes randomly chosen elements from the old Islamic architecture and sticks them on new buildings without any attempt at an integrated structure – a fault that many critics, rightly or wrongly, have also discerned in the New Classical idiom of architects such as Allan Greenberg.

Against that I make two claims: first, we cannot burden architecture with a prescribed mission to provide 'identity'. And second: we will not in this way achieve the pleasure and value that inheres in the architectural experience itself. Before examining those claims, I need to outline what I think to be the prevailing misconceptions about Islamic architecture.

First is the question of what exactly is Islamic architecture. When I was in college, professors used to ask us at least once a year to design a project in a 'Modernized Arabic Style'. What they meant was using the typical Islamic house design from the Ottoman, Ayyubid or Mamluk periods (of course without making any of those distinctions) – for instance, a rectangular or square building with a patio at its centre surrounded by arcades and punctuated by a water fountain – and adding such clichés as the *mashrabiya* (screened oriole window), vaulted rooms with wall niches and arched windows, not forgetting to top a few spaces with small domes or to divide summer from winter sections. The secret of how to modernize this mixture was to insert a curvature somewhere in the plan, or to rotate the upper floor at an angle from the lower one! The unfortunate thing was (and is) that the students were as ignorant about everything to do with that well-accomplished old style referred to as 'Islamic' as our professors were.

I didn't grasp the extent of this ignorance until I started my research, during which I carried out a survey on two hundred architecture students from different years, presenting them with a yes or no questionnaire about Islamic architecture. I asked, for example, if they thought that there was such a thing as 'contemporary Islamic architecture'; whether it expressed the *Zeitgeist*; whether they thought the old Islamic architecture expressed a certain conception; whether they felt that Western architecture was a threat to its existence. I also asked them to grade elements such as the patio, dome, *mashrabiya* and so on, and their importance to an overall design.

The results showed a shocking ignorance of the history of Islamic architecture and a complete sense of being at a loss as to what should be done. Moreover, the students exhibited the kind of 'group think' that is normally associated with stereotyping: in-group vs. out-group, Arabic vs. Western, etc., everything conceived in the context of a threat to identity and a need for self-assertion.

There were also deep, unexplained contradictions. For instance, 83% believed in the existence of contemporary or modern Islamic architecture, but 69% thought that it didn't express our *Zeitgeist* – in other words, it's modern but it doesn't express modernity; and 43% didn't know whether Islamic architecture had any underlying conception, yet 66% felt that Western architecture was a threat to national identity. Such attitudes are not restricted to the survey sample; they can be read quite easily in any research, literature or conference notes on the question of Islamic architecture, and more importantly in the buildings that are constructed under the influence of such thinking.

In my thesis I argued that the Arabic-speaking region (which was, until the fall of the Ottoman Empire, called the *ummah*) had, through architecture, defined itself as an in-group and sought to compensate for its lost identity by binding the channels of expression with stereotypes. In searching for an identity, it accentuated differences, e.g. Arab vs. West, but it thereby set the West up as an axis. 'Western' architectural accomplishments were subsequently either to be opposed or imitated, regardless of artistic or social requirements; and architects were hindered from setting out on the path of true self-discovery.

With regard to their own local architecture, there has been a fundamental confusion between 'traditional' and 'Islamic'. The first can be called 'local' or 'vernacular' and is quite distinct from the Islamic, not only because much of it has been built by people who were neither Muslims nor aspiring to be Muslims. True Islamic architecture, on the other hand, has a distinctive and distinguished architectural style that is easy for the expert to recognize (it cannot be reduced to a narrow group of elements; it encapsulates the entire architectural experience). Moreover, its architectural forms express an artistic intention that constrains the conscious choices of the architect. 'Traditional', on the other hand, denotes an unreflecting norm. It can be defined as the architecture of the local context, the 'instinctive' forms suggested by need, function and indigenous materials. Even if it includes aesthetic choices, they merely reflect the surrounding context.

The confusions between the two can be explained by the simple fact that Islamic architecture has formed part of that surrounding context for almost ten centuries. Moreover, the distinction is not a black and white one: the two overlap and interact, the traditional forming the background from which the Islamic style emerged as something consciously devoted to an idea, as opposed to the 'simplicity' of the forms lifted from the indigenous repertoire.

The 'traditional' styles have been experimented with by well-known contemporary Arabic architects such as Hassan Fathy, Mohamed Saleh Makiya, Abdel-Wahed El-Wakil, Rifat Chadirji and Rasem Badran. Despite the idiosyncracies of each of their architectural experiments, they all have something in common, which is the adoption of vernacular elements, and the acknowledgment that these exist and endure because they are adapted to context and climate. Despite what might look like an intertwining with the forms of Islamic architecture, their end-product is fundamentally different from true Islamic architecture, which is animated by Islamic moral choices, Islamic thought and an associated aesthetic.

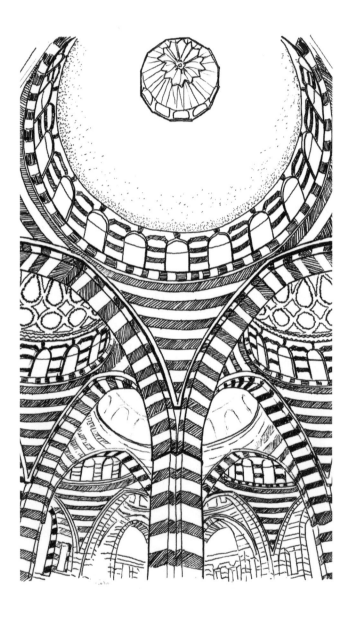

▲ An example of traditional architecture: New Baris Village,
designed by Hassan Fathy (interior).

◀ An example of Islamic architecture: Khan As'ad Pasha Al-Azm
in Damascus (interior).

This is additionally apparent from the literature produced by those architects and their like-minded followers. Fathy, for instance, never claimed to have any affinities with Islamic architecture, being inspired rather by vernacular mud buildings as well as by the ancient Sasanian architecture of Egypt (where the traditional Sasanian dome with its octagonal neck was adapted to indigenous Nubian patterns). Even when he used elements from the Islamic tradition, such as the dome or *mashrabiya*, he always attributed that use to passive design solutions to problems of climate or economics. More evidence can be found in his design approach, whether through his focus on constructional aspects and outward openness, or his dependence on the plan as starting point. Most importantly, the austerity of the resulting architectural experience is very far from the multi-layered response that is invited by the true Islamic way of building, in which an idea of God and the work of creation is expressed in every detail.

Nonetheless, Fathy's product is routinely confused with Islamic architecture, and in the circles in which I was educated the point was neither negotiable nor even debatable. When I likened his work to that of a village doctor who wears the hat of a scientist but never that of a creative artist, and whose concern is to raise his society from poverty and ignorance through practical measures, I was accused almost of heresy. My point was that Fathy used architecture as a means, not an end; hence his product should be judged in terms of its efficiency, not its meaning. One professor almost had a heart attack while insulting me in response. But I maintain that the same line of thought can be applied to the products of all the prominent practising architects mentioned above.

Controversy also surrounds the naming of Islamic architecture. There are notable nuances between 'Islamic', 'Moorish', 'Mohammedan', and similar. But the most prominent tension is between 'Islamic' and 'Arabic', which touches directly on the identity crisis that has formed the refrain to my discussions in this book. The struggle between 'Arabism' and Islam is a relatively new one, arising after Michel Aflaq, the founder of the Ba'ath party, promoted an Arabic identity in place of the Islamic one. But of course not all Arabs are Muslims, just as not all Muslims are Arabs. (Aflaq, for example, was an Orthodox Christian and conceived the idea of an 'Arab' identity while a student in Paris ... which does not mean – or does it? – that the idea of an Arab identity is a Western invention.) It must also be noted that Christian architects and builders have made a notable contribution to the history of Islamic architecture.

Naturally, given that after the Muslim conquests other religions became minorities in the Arabic-speaking world, it is inevitable that most significant building in that world was thereafter the work of Muslims. Nevertheless, we should not ignore the facts, such as that Sa'id Bin Kateb al-Faraghani, the architect of the Ibn Tulun mosque in Cairo, was a Christian,[1] or that architects and artisans of Armenian or Greek origin made important contributions under the Ottomans. Mimar Sinan, responsible for over three hundred of the most important buildings in the great period of Ottoman architecture in the sixteenth century, and the designer of the standard Islamic school, or *madrasa*, was from an Orthodox Christian family, and rose through the ranks of the largely Christian Janissaries to become the leading architect of his day.

The Orientalist writer Titus Burckhardt has discussed the validity of the term 'Arabic architecture', bringing into focus the two aspects, Islam and Arabism. Although Islam is an 'open invitation' to everyone and not a 'racial phenomenon' in Burckhardt's terms, the Arabic language is still a critical element of the faith. For every Muslim, whether Arab or not, the language of the Koran is essential, both for praying and for reading the Holy Book. The language is not only a spoken tongue; it is also a mode of thinking. As Burckhardt writes, 'Arabic determined to a greater or less degree the "style of thinking" of all Muslim people',[2] and this was reflected in all their other forms of expression, including architecture and art.

Nevertheless, despite this marriage between the religion and the language that introduced it, there is no reason to regard the two as equivalent. 'It would, indeed, be impossible to confine the manifestations of Islam to Arabism; on the contrary, it is Arabism that was expanded and, as it were, transfigured by Islam.'[3] Burckhardt's meaning is that what Islam gave to Arabism cannot be compared to what Arabism gave back.

This returns me to the 'accomplishment' concept discussed in the previous chapter. There is a real Islamic accomplishment: the worldwide promulgation of a faith, with all the ideas and beauty that pertain to that faith, including a monumental architectural achievement manifesting itself in great buildings – libraries, schools, mosques, hammams, khans, souks –built with a great sense of detail and morality, and a potent display of the range of that civilization. By comparison, there is no Arabist accomplishment that can remotely match this. Arabic itself has been preserved and developed by the Koran, but for which book this now widely proliferated language would have disappeared long ago; and the best proof of that is the way in which the myriad dialects of the region have been unified through the sacred text that they share.

Moreover, describing our region's architecture as 'Arabic' excludes from the equation those who enriched Islamic architecture most effectively: namely the Persians, Seljuks, Moguls and Ottomans. Islamic architecture reached the peak of its glory under what architectural historians call the three Empires: Safavid, Ottoman and Indian Mogul. Hence, the term 'Islamic' is validated by the fact that this architecture is the outward manifestation and expression of a civilization and a faith.[4] Even the term 'Islamic architecture' has caused confusion and led to stereotyping when understood as the *architecture of Islam*. The architecture that was produced from the eighth century until the late seventeenth century, from the tail end of Umayyad rule until the decline of the Ottoman Empire, and that was spread from Mogul India to Morocco and Andalusia, was not an architecture of religion but the result of that religion on people who believed in and lived through it. So although it has manifested the Islamic conceptions of the people who produced it, it remains as *their* understanding, *their* interaction, and should not be understood as an architecture based on Islamic law or anything like that.

Using such loose terms as 'traditional', 'original', 'Arabic' and so on, and incorporating them into stereotypes, becomes a way of mere labelling instead of analytical understanding. By this labelling certain randomly chosen elements are detached from any attempt to understand the whole architectural experience, in order to see architecture as a means to the unjustified end of 'identity'. Architectural criticism is thereby rejected in favour of identity politics. The surprising thing is that this entire labelling process is done *collectively*, through group behaviour directed at maintaining an ideological orthodoxy.

The result is an inability to produce any new architecture, while remaining in the closed circle, searching for the lost self, and misunderstanding, misusing and distorting our once great architectural history. This endless pursuit of one's own tail deprives architects of the freedom of aesthetic choice and design invention. It pushes them towards one of two practices: either blindly imitating 'Western' architecture as produced by architects working without reference to peers or competing architectural ideals, or else entering the dead-end of pastiche and collage. Key questions are raised by this discussion: What are the elements that define our architecture, and how are they used in local practice? And what is the 'right' architectural experience, and how can it be achieved?

In answer to the first set of questions my own exploration of the literature, and my encounters with architects, clients and the ordinary people of our country, suggest that the label 'Islamic' is confined to the following basic elements: dome, patio, *mashrabiya*, *muqarnas* (i.e. honeycomb vaulting), minaret, geometric patterns and Arabic calligraphy. However, although all of these elements were to be found in the old Islamic buildings, each has a different use, timeline and source – facts that are altogether ignored or misinterpreted in current practice. Old Islamic architecture benefited from the context in which it arose. It did not begin from a *tabula rasa*, but made use of an existing heritage, reproducing, reinventing and imposing its individual stamp on vernacular architecture, until the connection with the original source became almost undetectable.

By understanding the basic tenets of the Islamic style, we can grasp the enormity of the misuse that is being practised now in the name of 'inspiration' and 'identity'. To understand this would enable us to take more *pleasure* from those works, and more importantly help us to make connections with the past that would be a matter of rational choice rather than mere distorted copying. Those tenets of course cannot be seen in any written law, in documents by historians or in the memoirs of ancient architects because such things have not been found. However, they are a common thread noticed and verified by many scholars, even if they are still 'readings' and not to be counted as certainties.

The Arabic language and monotheism are the two most essential tenets. They are like the thread of a rosary, whose different beads of various sizes and colours are the multicultural expressions of those two commanding tenets. It is possible to distinguish the different effects of different languages on periods of Islamic architecture, starting with the 'imaginative intuition' of the Arabic language in contrast to the 'auditive intuition' of Latin languages.[5]

A sense of the dynamic is generated by the 'tree of verbal forms' that is a distinctive feature of Arabic. Each verb consists of three invariable constants, but as many as twelve different verbal modes spring from these constants, each producing in turn different forms of nouns and adjectives, all nonetheless linking back to the initial verb form. Thus the tree has the dynamic ability to produce an infinity of new expressions from a single root idea. However,

Arabic also has a static aspect. This can be seen, for example, in the nominal sentence, which juxtaposes nouns irrespective of time. The intertwining of the dynamic and the static can be read in devices of Islamic art such as the arabesque, in which rhythm and order are fully expressed and intertwined, the monotony of repetition being broken with 'rhythmic alternation' and 'qualitative perfection of each element'.

Contrasting the 'incisive and dynamic' Arabic with the 'all-embracing and circumspect' Turkish, or the language of the Persian for whom 'Unity manifests itself above all as harmony', Burckhardt displays differences as corresponding to distinct 'mental types' and resulting in distinct art forms. '[The Turk's] works always proceed out of an all-enveloping concept; they are as if hewn from a single block,' while the Persian's 'inner melody' and 'hierarchical gradations' result in architectural articulation and accord.

At the same time, the architectural manifestations of the Arabic language's mental type derive from the higher source of this language in the Koran, in which style is developed to an unassailable perfection. Hence, Burckhardt's conclusion that 'there's no such thing as Quranic style which can simply be transposed into art, but there does exist a state of soul which is sustained by the recitation of the Quran and which favors certain formal manifestations while precluding others'.

The effect of the intertwining of dynamics and statics – the creation and resolution of tension, as manifested in architectural and artistic forms – has been described by scholars as Divine Unity, or the Unity of Existence, which is assimilated to *tawhid*, the oneness of God. This is the essential notion of Islam and the key message of the Koran: 'There is no God but the one and only God.' These scholars have read the principle of 'Unity in multiplicity, and multiplicity in unity' in each layer of the many layers that compose the old Islamic works, both in the elements of space and in the decoration that is used to enhance it.

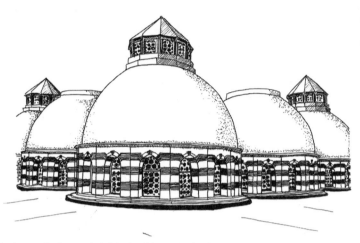

▲ An example of an exterior in Islamic architectural style: Khan As'ad Pasha Al-Azm in Damascus.

▼ A contrasting example of an exterior in traditional architectural style: New Baris Village, designed by Hassan Fathy.

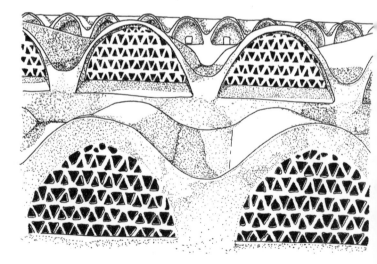

Most old Islamic buildings – particularly residential or civic – lack a central space, being composed of sequenced and juxtaposed parts. Some critics have condemned this idiom as making the building, when compared with the traditions of composition in the West, unreadable from a single vantage point. That view regards the focus in Islamic architecture as concentrated on the interior, so that it is the exterior rather than the interior that is 'hidden'.[6]

The reason for this kind of composition is that succeeding rulers inherited the job of continuing buildings that had yet to be completed, adding new additions organically, without reference to a master plan. This is exactly what provoked the French mandate in Damascus and other Syrian cities to 'correct' the fabric of our organic cities, by making clearances around key monuments, as mentioned in Chapter 3. In fact the sequenced approach and openness to horizontal growth pervaded the whole of an architectural work, down to the smallest detailing on the interior, and resulted, on the outside, in a humane urbanization of the surroundings and a lived experience of deep settlement. We are talking here of the way in which a building that prays and invites the Almighty into the city also extends its gentle hands around its neighbourhood, to create a zone of day-to-day peace.

A Christian church is oriented from west to east, directing the perceiver along a single main axis to focus on what is most important and sacred, this effect being enhanced by the fact that all motion and all descending light converge on the altar. By contrast, the space of a mosque is dominated by unity on all levels. There is no veneration of any universal object, and no differentiation between one person and another. Hence, the order of the space is open and united, and the eye can rest calmly in equilibrium without turning in any specific direction. Even when (as is the case with many Syrian monuments) a building consists of layers of older architectural works, such as the Umayyad Great Mosque in Damascus – first a pagan temple, then the Roman Temple of Jupiter,

▲ Christian-style rib vault.

▼ Islamic-style rib vault.

then the Christian cathedral of John the Baptist, before becoming a mosque – differences can be seen in the organization of space. In the case of the Great Mosque, scholars such as Burckhardt have detected an openness towards the courtyard, in contrast to the introverted space of Roman churches; and an internal space that expresses an 'undifferentiated plenitude' manifested by the 'synthesis of stability and abundance' in the repeated rows of sweeping two-storey columns and arcades. This design is deliberate and intended to create peacefulness in the soul, resting the eye through lightness and stability, and soothing the worshipper in the presence of the Almighty.

Many of the space elements that were used in Islamic architecture were of course also used in Christian architecture, such as vaults and cupolas. However, Islamic architecture managed to reproduce them in a completely different way, from the point of view of both meaning and technique. For instance, one might compare Persian (Islamic) and Gothic (Christian) rib vaults. The different segments of a Persian vault are presented as facets of a single concave surface, the intersecting ribs not converging at the crown but rather leaving the central cupola free. In contrast, the Gothic vault's converging powers seem to ascend from the supporting columns upwards to the joint that is present at the crown. In this regard, it might be seen that architectural differences correspond to spiritual differences between the two religions, although they are not differences of essence so much as differences of *emphasis.*[7] The 'union with God', which is a central theme in Christianity, corresponds to the upward striving of its architecture. By contrast, the dropping-down embracing unity of Islam can be read in *its* architecture: an inherent unity, from which the 'component elements' are deduced, and which is not produced from those elements by any upward visual dynamic.

Differences of static order between Classical European architecture and Islamic architecture may also be seen. The first adulated the human body as the image of God, and this was reflected in the weight distribution and building statics as a proportioning of the building to its support: the building must, in the end, stand as we do. In the Islamic tradition, however, where adulation is permitted only towards the creating divinity, the logic becomes 'objectively static but never anthropomorphic'.[8] The mosque does not stand as we do: the blessings of the most high, brought down through worship, need no support from earthly things.

Unity in Islam is also expressed through decoration, which, contrary to the mainstream Western view of it as an over-used two-dimensional excess, is another manifestation of the inherited spiritual and moral vision of the faith. Through decoration, unity is expressed by blurring boundaries, so that nothing is truly individual save the One who is All. Decoration is not only used as a surface covering; it is also used to 'transform space', by covering structural elements and dissolving the barriers between the load-bearing and ornamental parts, thereby achieving fluidity, smoothing transitions and eliminating tensions. As the writer Dalu Jones has noted: 'Like water itself, which plays such a unique role in Islamic architecture, the decoration continually reflects and multiplies patterns to provide a "cool" refuge for the eye and the mind, creating an art that is dynamic yet unchanging.'[9]

Moreover, decoration also functions to confuse the eye by creating a game of interchangeability between the various elements and their original functions. 'There is, too, an inherent ambivalence in Islamic designs. An abstract curving shape can be read as a bird; calligraphy is decorative as well as being a message conveying a precise meaning. The lines in a primary grid of a façade, as in certain arabesques or in Abbasid woodcarving, transform a decorative element into the contour of form. The same designs are reproduced side by side in different materials and for different purposes.'[10]

The grids referred to are another contributing factor in creating unity, order and harmony, and they play a key role in a pleasing architectural experience. Islamic decoration had certain design principles, one of which was obedience to overall controlling grids. These map out the main elements of a decorative scheme, such as calligraphic bands, arches and niches, by which a surface is subdivided and the elements of the façade held visually together. Additional secondary grids map out the patterning within each of the elements of the primary grid, though they are generally imperceptible, existing only as underlying matrixes of squares, triangles, octagons or hexagons.

Such subtleties are only a small fraction of what has been studied and what still needs further study in the great history of Islamic architecture. But they give a general idea of what is being missed out by the modern approach, in which shadows and fragments of the past are pasted together without any conception of their meaning as parts of a whole. I am not in favour of mystical interpretations (some scholars seem sometimes to invoke a Sufi spirit that prefers poetic projections to concrete perceptions). Whether valid or not in themselves, these correspond to no physical details in the built form, and more importantly cannot add to or take away from the architectural experience. The question now is whether what has been described above of the aesthetics and spirit of Islamic architecture corresponds, however remotely, to what is being practised in the Arabic and Islamic regions today.

A key problem is the way in which existing elements have been exploited. Rarely are they now read in terms of their history. Thus the dome has become a cliché to be included in every building that seeks to have an 'Islamic' character, whether a mosque or public building, whether built by a Western or an Arabic practice, whether present or merely implied. In fact this particular element, originally found in Mesopotamia, dates back to 4000 BC, and was favoured for its structural properties. In old Islamic architecture the use of the dome was less frequent, with long and distant interruptions. Its use in mosques originates with the Dome of the Rock in Jerusalem, which adopted the Byzantine style before Islam had developed its own architectural language; likewise with the cupola of the Umayyad Great Mosque in Damascus (706–715 AD). The dome as an element was not regarded as essential until the Seljuks embraced its use in the eleventh century. It was later fully developed by Mimar Sinan as the central space of the mosque, inspired in this case by the Byzantine architecture of Hagia Sofia in Istanbul. However, although Sinan had been charmed by Hagia Sofia's dome space, he dedicated his work to experiment, so as to develop a dome-style of his own – almost certainly studying Michelangelo's plans for St Peter's in Rome.

It is therefore surprising that the dome is today regarded as a required element in every mosque building; and all the more shameful that it is so often simply deposited on top of a finished structure like a hat. It is the same story with the element most dear to the identity seekers: the *mashrabiya*, which reached the climax of its use in residential Ottoman architecture, being a solution to the problem of reconciling one's own privacy with the need to peer out over the privacy of others – the perfect gossip-feeding device. But to use it today in order to 'dress identity' is no better than stereotyping, without any real architectural sense. The same critique can be made of the patio, the *muqarnas*, the minaret, the geometric patterning and Arabic calligraphy identified by my research as the key elements in Islamic architecture. Each element has been well studied by historians, and it is known that none was used with the veneration and adulation that are bestowed on them today; none was regarded as a central idea, rather than a decorative by-product of the architectural process; and most definitely none was a tool for achieving any separate goal or loaded agenda.

So much for indigenous usage of the key elements today. As regards Western usage, one needs only to look at project briefs and promotional literature from well-known Western architects who have been active in the Arabic regions (mostly the Gulf), such as

Norman Foster and Henning Larsen. On every possible occasion they claim to be 'taking inspiration from traditional Islamic architecture' or 'communicating with traditional elements' and so on. Modern architects seem to feel obliged to sell their product as having some special connection with history generally, and with the history of the place they are about to desecrate specifically. Maybe this is because they are aware of the radical break with the history of mankind that is represented by their way of building, and are thus hoping to gain by their words the approval that they can never win by their deeds.

The only problem is that they are attributing the wrong labels to architectural history: confusing the traditional with the Islamic. Moreover they are thereby claiming historical justification to build in one place using forms that belong to another – something particularly noticeable in the Gulf, whose architectural heritage is so limited and sparse, it having been largely desert with no developed urban centres before the discovery of petroleum beneath the sands. But the most intrusive thing is the way these so-called affinities are exploited, in architecture that has been dropped into the desert from outer space, or at any rate from cyber space, since it is for the most part designed on the computer, like the bubbles and gadgets of Zaha Hadid. No process of exchanging data and twisting forms can substitute for the architect, whose role must be to direct the whole building's atmosphere: the games of light and shadow, the movement of the eye, the effect of sounds .... Rather than simply achieving the impact of theatrical volumes, the focus must be on considering the entire architectural experience.

Architects know that they ought to achieve identity with the place where they are building, otherwise their architecture will look less like a city and more like a shelf of perfume bottles, as in Dubai. But, as I have argued, identity cannot be achieved as a prescribed recipe. It is not an independent goal of design, but a by-product of designing meaningfully and beautifully, according to the spirit of the place.

We should ask ourselves whether Western architects practising in the Arabic regions are the only ones to blame for the meaningless buildings we see there? And should they only take the blame for the sprayed-on pieces of 'traditional inspiration' or the brushstrokes of 'traditional' elements, and not for the rest of what they do? With *what* is the architect going to communicate in his architecture, and how come the architectural scene in these countries has become dominated by architects who are foreign to their intimate understanding of life and the universe? If these places were 'filled' with such an understanding, then empty architectural gestures would have no place. Hence the desperate clinging to 'fillers' from the past in order to disguise the Swiss cheese structure of our communities and their built environment. Why is the history of Islamic architecture emptied of all meaning and aesthetic sense? Those questions correspond directly with my original questions: what determines the right architectural experience, and how can it have meaning and be judged?

Roger Scruton writes in *The Aesthetics of Architecture*: 'The fulfilment of a rational agent – what the Greeks called *eudaimonia* and we happiness – comes only when the agent has that which he values, as opposed to that which he merely desires. And perhaps the most striking feature of the "architecture of human need" is that it seems so often to conceive the world as a world in which there *are* no values, but only animal needs – fresh air, health, exercise, food.'[11] To this another scale of need must be added, which is sustainability: nowadays architecture needs to sell its product in terms of how much energy it conserves and what ecological impact it has.

Undoubtedly needs have a fundamental part to play in the design process. But we must consider their status in this process, and how they have become both the focus that controls the architect's choices and the standard whereby those choices must be judged.

While human needs are universal and must be addressed, the values that underpin decision-making in design are more complex and culturally specific. Our sense of value, as Scruton explains it, can be educated through rational discussion, and is rooted in our wider moral and spiritual concerns. It is not reducible to the 'functional' goals of a building (using the term 'functional' in the narrow sense of a practical program). Through discussion and comparison, values become the foundation on which 'bridges of logic' can be constructed from one taste to another. And from here what is central to the architectural experience can be recaptured: 'We must then search for that core of experience ... in which we find ourselves reflected, not as creatures of the moment, consumed in the present activity, but as rational beings, with a past, a present and a future.'[12]

The stability of the value doesn't mean the unchangeability of the product, but its adaptability to the larger human picture. Values are preferences: 'Our preference means something more to us than mere pleasure or satisfaction. It is the outcome of thought and education; it is expressive of moral, religious and political feelings, of an entire *Weltanschauung*, with which our identity is mingled.'[13]

But what should the fulcrum of the logical discussion be, by which architectural experience can be adjusted and improved? According to Scruton, the matter can be addressed in two aspects, visual pleasure and moral values: '[My argument] seemed to suggest that criticism involves a search for the "correct" or "balanced" perception, the perception in which ambiguities are resolved and harmonies established, allowing the kind of pervasive visual satisfaction which I hinted at. But that cannot be all. The conceptions which influence our experience of architecture are as far-reaching as the conceptions which govern our lives.'[14]

This aesthetic understanding cannot be reached *in advance* of the architectural experience, derived from a set of rules or a *prescribed* form of knowledge; rather it is the result of an intuitive engagement in the experience offered by the building. This engagement happens on two levels of perception: the primitive and the rational. The primitive level is the first impression that inclines the perceiver to describe his experience with words such as 'serene', 'welcoming, or 'stimulating': on this level the visual pleasure results from what the building offers the eye, and how and where it makes the eye move. On the rational level, pleasure results from understanding what has been perceived as appropriate and right, through an engaged 'process of contemplation and comparing'. This engaged form of contemplation, Scruton argues, can be understood through the question 'why'. 'Why does a thing look a certain way?', 'why does this detail make me feel a certain feeling?' and 'why did the architect/designer choose to do things this way rather than another?'. This question 'why?' is what I vainly tried to address with my superiors in the architecture department, and which they persisted in understanding as a threat. But it is, surely, the foundation of perceptive appreciation.

The true aesthetic way resists the burden of an explicit message; rather the perceiver should be able to feel what Scruton calls 'the inward resonance of an idea or a way of life'. This can only be reached through experiencing the embodiment of the moral life in every detail of the building and in its manner of production. Not an imposed moral lesson, but an inwardness with the moral sympathies of the observer: 'The experience of Chartres is the apprehension of a divine light penetrating all things, of matter made permeable to Soul, of a universal harmony which transforms every stone from its material roughness into a minute symbol of the intellectual love of God.'[15]

Only in this way does the perceiver enter the inner world of the building: 'One does not learn about medieval theology from Chartres: but one does learn what it is like to believe in it, what it is like to see and feel the world as the people of Chartres once saw and felt it.'[16]

The perceiver has a key role in the architectural experience. Aesthetic characteristics are latent in a building, and have to be activated through 'imaginative perception'. What has been articulated by the architect is imagined in the mind of the perceiver: for example, the way that a sequence of steps gives the impression of ascendance, or a series of columns the impression of an infinite path. This happens both primitively, where the perceiver has no control over what he perceives, and on a deeper level rationally, when the perceiver chooses to get more engaged in the architectural experience.

While the perceiver has the role of distinguishing what is to be felt and observed in the building, how is the architect to coordinate this experience of meaning? Different approaches use the terms 'dynamic structure'[17] and 'universal structure'[18] to explain how, through its formal order, a building communicates with the perceiver.

One example of both structures is the willow tree. Why does the observer perceive this as sad? The answer might be because the way the tree dangles its branches downwards seems like a loss of will, a sad drooping of being. There is an isomorphism between the structure of the tree and the structure of the feeling.[19]

One can also perceive a universal structure without concomitant feelings. A door, for example, is perceived firstly as a door, before any conscious perception of its size, colour or any other formal characteristics. Its 'door-ness' is the result of what is known collectively about objects of this nature.[20]

The formal ('universal') structure of the willow tree or the door generates perceptions associated with and logically consistent with that specific structure. But we can also perceive these structures imaginatively ('dynamically'), bringing to them our past experience, our background knowledge, our degree of intelligence, and other psychological, social and cultural factors. In this regard there is inter-reliance between the perceiver's background and the universal structures.

However, I would suggest that there is a slight difference between the willow and the door examples. The universal structure of the first is unchangeable, being part of a world humans had no hand in creating, and belonging to the inescapable background to our ideas and designs. 'Door-ness', however, is the creation of humans and although it has not been radically changed since it was created, and although it corresponds in one way or another with other natural 'doors' in the universe (such as cave openings or tree holes), its universal structure is changeable, unlike that of the willow tree. As an architect or designer I can ask myself questions such as: why do I need this 'door'? What is the function (in the wide sense of the word) of a door?

Such questions can alter the universal structure of the door by creating different versions of it and thus radically altering the concept of 'door-ness'. Door-ness is not perceived as a natural essence, unlike the willow-ness of the willow tree. Of course, I will not be able to escape the universal structure entirely because man cannot create *ab initio* – he merely reassembles what occurs around him. If I want to defy the universal structure for a door, however, I might research doors around me, such as the 'doors' in the human body, even on the cellular level, or in a volcano or a river. Thus I might imagine a door being developed as a permeable membrane, in which case 'door-ness' as we currently apprehend it (a rectangular aperture that can be opened and closed) is eradicated and the 'universal structure' is altered – unlike that of a tree, which is an unescapable natural creation. My point is that the universal structures of human products are less resilient than those of any natural object, since we ourselves had a part in shaping them. In contrast with the created universe, what we humans have made is always questionable and we always have the issue of its appropriateness or rightness. With any tool or device that we make, we strive, as Scruton explains, to 'give a sense of what it means, by filling in the background of expectations, customs and attitudes against which it is deployed'.[21]

In daily life, when aiming at what is appropriate, we adopt a 'problem-solving' formula, searching for the means to some given end. What is appropriate is explored both before and after the action is performed. Architects must also seek to fit their deeds appropriately and successfully to a given context. However, the wider aim must be to create something of lasting value, not a quick solution to a current assignment. The aim must be to produce something that has meaning not simply for us here and now, but for all who encounter it, both now and so long as it lasts.

This cultivation of our sense of the appropriate must therefore establish connections between aesthetic characteristics and our moral/social life. Scruton considers the moral sense to derive from our response to each other as social creatures, joined to an order greater than each person's individual ego. This moral sense can seem radically different from place to place and culture to culture, especially in its application to the things that we make: an object or a building can speak with welcome accents to one person, while being repellent to another. However, everything we do raises the question of its acceptability to others, and this is as true of architecture as it is of all our words and deeds. It belongs to human nature to pursue agreement in things that matter, and to reconcile our interests through a system of rights and duties. Hence we humans stand in need of a foundation, a system of law, through which we can address each other and to which we can appeal in our conflicts.

This is what is provided, we Muslims believe, in Islamic law, as derived from the Koran and the hadiths. This system of law is not – as so many Westerners seem to believe, and as so many so-called Muslims seem to want them to believe – a set of absolutist edicts that extinguish freedom and discussion. On the contrary, it is an instrument of reconciliation, by which interests are sifted and rights assigned, so as to resolve the conflicts that are inherent in human communities.[22]

It is not the remit of this book to pursue the deep question of universal law, with all its philosophical and theological ramifications. The point is that, with or without that law, human beings are in need of rational argument, and must cultivate a sense of the right and the appropriate if they are really to know what they are doing. This is as true of architecture as it is of everyday behaviour. When the sense of the appropriate orders our experience, and we witness Alberti's 'correspondence of part with part, and the part with the whole', this guarantees the pleasure of the eye and its movement within a frame of visual validity. The 'moral life,' as Scruton writes, '*ennobles our choices*'; the beautiful work of architecture shows 'an accumulation of moral character, it wears a sympathetic expression… and *inhabits the same world as the man who passes it*'.[23]

On the other hand, an object or a building can become alien to humans when it fails to invite the perceiver to understand and to relate to it. Buildings that do not 'bear the imprint of what is appropriate' stand in an alienated relation to people. And this is what we saw in the architectural crimes described in previous chapters.

The embodiment of moral life was achieved brilliantly in some of the old works of Islamic architecture. These works excelled in creating multi-layered correspondences so that, for all the richness of detail, the eye and mind would never become bored or exhausted. Zooming in from the harmonized whole, unwrapping the interwoven layers of space, elements, pattern, light and water, the eye can move in small sequenced rebounds from eye to mind and back again. On any 'layer' on which the eye settles, the mind is invited to follow it, into an arena of pleasurable and meaningful experience. Think of a tree as an example. You can enjoy the shape of the tree, the smell, the shade. You can enhance your experience and take it to a deeper level if you wish: you can focus on its bark, on the insects that march on it, on the tiny details that make up each leaf and each line. All these layers are combined to make up the 'soul' of the tree. On each level of experience there is a new world of 'design' to be discovered and enjoyed. It is exactly that effect at which the old Islamic architecture aimed.

There can also be amazement, or what is known today as 'the wow factor'. This wow-ness is what many modern works aim at. The only problem is that if wow-ness is not accompanied by a sense of meaning it soon fades away, leading to the feeling of alienation. Pleasure and meaning must be in balance, just like the eye-mind movement controlled by moral thought. That is the key difference, from my point of view, between the buildings of today and the buildings of yesterday. Those of the past *layered* their beauty, starting with the building material and carrying through to the very last detail, all in the service of one harmonized experience. Pleasure in such a building is a continuous experience of revelation, instead of a single hammer strike on the head!

Yesterday, the ground of belief was not as slippery as it is today. Whether Greek, Roman, Buddhist, Gothic, Islamic or even Aztec or Pharaonic, this stability of belief (from ancient days until recent history) ordered what was appropriate in moral life, and this order was subsequently carried over into style and a sense of identity. Architecture has moved with the shifting of those beliefs to a point where it resorts to 'ritualization'.[24] That is what we see in the case of the cut-and-paste approach: 'Although classical architecture initially evolved from a stylistic repertoire similar to that of any indigenous tradition, its forms have become increasingly disassociated from their original meanings.'[25]

Alternatively, architecture resorts to the complete abandonment of any continuity, or recognition of the human need for settlement and home, as in so much modern architecture, where new tenets are being invented to give meaning to aesthetic choices, but without any conception of, or respect towards, the people on whom those choices are to be imposed. This was the pattern set by Le Corbusier in his inhuman plans for Paris and Algiers, and also by Ecochard and Banshoia in Damascus.

It is a pattern that has too often been followed by those educated in Western schools of architecture, and by those who have so frequently been brought in as practitioners or consultants in the Middle East. It is also a fall-back for those Middle Eastern intellectuals who, in resenting religion, resent what they perceive as the accomplishment of Islamic architecture (and thus reject it or seek to disguise its identity). Modern architecture prefers to control a place, rather than to respect it. And in order to achieve full control it gives us vast gadgets, designed on a computer, that bear no relation to the real needs, both moral and spiritual, of the people.

The problem is that humans have lost control over what they are trying to achieve, and because this loss of control is being ignored they try to compensate through wow-ness or through using a stipulated repertoire peeled off the back of the past. I have tried to point to the deficiencies in architectural education, research and building in my country and in other countries of our region, but the fact is that these regions don't have any orientation anymore; we don't share the Western scientific approach towards the universe and we definitely haven't adopted the tools to implement this.

We also stand on religious and moral grounds that have been thoroughly undermined. There is a state of intractability, with no willingness either to engage in the battle to overcome the universe materially and all that that would mean by way of hard work, or to commit to spiritual beliefs that require no less sacrifice and hard work than the materialist alternative. We have sought the best of the two worlds with the least amount of hardship, and for this greed we are punished by the loss of our true home. Surrendering our major architectural projects to Western expertise is no less of a mistake because we relieve ourselves thereby of the burden of asking the real questions. Those questions are ours, and we must try to answer them, if we are not to lose ourselves in the futile and cruel conflicts over 'identity' that have destroyed this whole part of our world.

Of course nothing of what I have discussed above found ears willing to listen at the university. I argued that we must give up the retro approach of using the past as a quarry of fragments; in response

I was accused of despising history and subverting our inheritance. I tried to explain that stereotyping burdens architecture with an imposed message that denies its inner vitality. I criticized the habit of creating certain shapes whenever the term 'Islamic' is used, and the complete waste of resources on spurious demands such as identity which should arise from our moral understanding and not from clichés and stereotypes. I asked for freedom of vision, and in response was treated as if I were joining the demonstrations for freedom outside. I asked for a deeper exploration of the practice of the past, not just the resulting form but also the thought that produced it, so I was looked on as though a member of ISIS and a terrorist threat. In the discussions with the judging panel, when I was finally granted permission to defend my thesis, I was faced with the most disconnected and extraneous questions, such as 'how can I pull the stereotype off one building and paste it on another?' or 'why are there only ten books listed in your bibliography?'. The discussion was at times more like an interrogation: 'I will talk and you be quiet; never answer my questions!', 'The proof that architecture is not an art is that the faculty carries the name of an architectural engineer; and engineering is not an art!'

These remarks came from professors who also run private universities and plan a considerable part of our cities. I was standing up against them with the support only of my professor, who knew as well as I did that it was impossible for me to attain this degree without him backing me every step of the way. Because he was a Christian at least my research could not be prosecuted in the improvised 'terrorism court'; our partnership, to say the least, confused our opponents and often made them lose their temper.

It was a mystery to them how this great man could help me to get all my papers proofed and delivered by hand, working as a buffer between me and them. He invited me to his home and sometimes to his in-laws' to discuss the work when there was no way to move safely in the streets. We met on the sidewalk or in the back of a car when mortars and snipers were showering our skies. His wife lit a candle for me at church, and he prayed for me to triumph over the injustice and cruelty that I had unwittingly provoked, merely by allowing myself to think. He faced all their obstinacy and hostility with reason and wisdom, and tried to deflect as much as he could away from me and onto himself.

They had done everything they could to delay my work for almost two years. It didn't matter that my husband and I were almost killed trying to get to the university through the only remaining route from our home. It didn't matter either if there was no electricity for three days running, and I had to read and translate by candlelight; it didn't matter if there had been no water in the city for a week; it didn't matter if I had spent the night sleeping on the floor to cool off, or had dressed in everything I owned to keep warm. Even if they were enduring the same hardships, I didn't expect them to go easy on me; nor did I even want them to treat me in the same corrupt way they treated everybody else. I could cope with their demands for projects to be printed out despite the lack of electricity (so a student had to locate a suitable shop that had a functioning power generator) and the lack of supplies (there was scarcely a functional printer that had not been looted, and even then its owner would have to be skilled at liquefying mixed ink). I could cope with paying the shop owner as much as he wished to charge for providing such a coveted service, and I could cope with meeting the unreasonable deadlines issued by the professors. I could also cope with the fact that a project might – regardless of the actual work in it – be rejected for not being 'neat' enough. Now all I wanted was the chance to convene for a discussion in which my work would be finally judged.

The events of the day of my defence, when it was at last held – for no other reason than that my professor had blocked all excuses – are still vivid in my mind. After many heated rounds of delay and harassment, the date was set and the mandatory invitation cards were distributed. My professor and my husband had done their best to breathe some enthusiasm in me to stand the next day on the rostrum and display my pre-rejected ideas in another (hopefully final) encounter with deaf ears. I received a phone call hours before the seminar. My professor on the other end spoke with the tone he used whenever he was unsure how to deliver bad news, but this time he sounded as if he were mourning a death. I couldn't believe it: the same head of design who had been leading the fight had managed to get a note for postponement. This time he had run out of the so-called 'legal' manipulations, and as a result had played an illegal card.

I could barely contain myself. Then I received another call from someone who was playing the role of an 'intermediary', whose task was to see that things wouldn't explode. But I was exploding: I told him that I no longer wanted this degree, that I refused any other 'palliative' step, and that I was going to every TV channel and form of social media to expose what they were doing to me, and I would challenge all the professors in the university to a public debate. Of course the effect of such acts in that war-ruled reality would have been, to say the least, questionable, but for some reason my threats had an impact. That night all the odds worked in my favour. The head of design and the scientific vice president both received notes from the ministry in Damascus that demoted them from their administrative positions to educational ones. Luckily for me they believed that I had something to do with it. But the truth is that I had no idea why this had happened.

The next morning I went to the university together with my family and professor, my eyes puffy from crying. My professor wiped the gloating smiles off his colleagues' faces by showing them the written decision to hold the defence. They all stayed in their offices in a tacit boycott, while the panel who had been forced to convene sat to discuss the thesis. I was granted my PhD, and I watched my professor's eyes fill with tears as he looked back at me and said, 'We did it!'

In the end, my battle is a very humble one compared to the battles that have been fought and are still being fought by many trying to hold on to their positions: people suffering torture, injustice and maltreatment, wounds, illnesses and ordeals in so-called hospitals. My journey is put into perspective when considering those who faced debasement for a kilo of oranges or a few potatoes, or those who entered prison and endured the unendurable. Who am I beside the countless women who have lost their children to a stray bullet or to blind revenge, who have had to invent each day a new way to cope and provide, and who wake up every morning to do what they have to do without expecting anyone to give them thanks or even to listen to the story of their ordeals? Who am I next to the person who goes every day through security checkpoints to find work, knowing that every time he might never come back? Who am I next to a tailor who spends his day behind his sewing-machine holding a flashlight in his mouth, in order to fix in the dark old clothes that have been patched over and over again? Who am I in front of the person who spends her entire night queuing to buy bread that she might or might not get? Who am I in front of a child opening his eyes onto a classroom floor, or even the darkness of a pitiless prison? Who am I, and who is anyone at all, in front of the person who has persevered against an unbearable bitterness knowing that no one except himself has the task of finding meaning in it?

Yes, all around us we find the people who inspire us with the examples they set. A man who witnessed his brother burn to death due to a mortar shell and lay beside him on the pavement while drips of flaming fuel burned his own head and hands, watching a stunned street looking back at him and waiting for a neighbour to come to smother his flaming body with their own; with those burnt hands he still paints walls with a smile on his face. Such people – and there are many – help us to dream of a country that we can call home again. Those people are surviving on the very little that was left for them of the small businesses, spiritual beliefs, and mutilated urban and social fabric. It is worn out, yes, but still it struggles to survive, because good people give it life from their own precious fund.

Today, we have seen the outcome of our socialist system of five-year plans, and all the corruption that was inevitably involved in their implementation. We have seen the result in administration, education and moral life. We have seen the unbalance that they have created demographically and from their imposed zoning of all areas of human life. Imported solutions haven't done us any good either, whether intrusive such as a foreign occupation, or invited in order to 'show us how things should be done'.

If anything can be learned from this pointless war it is that our solutions should spring from our own depths; and that we should clean out those depths, whether the gutters have been built before our eyes or within the darkest corners of our souls. And, in the work of healing, architecture is as important as anything else we might do. We cannot heal merely by replacing our informal slums with faceless towers, whether these are designed by the military construction institution or by some starchitect in his air-conditioned office.

Our need is for a shared home, and this home must be ours, built from our sense of who we are as citizens of this place, and from our wish to restore it, to embellish it, to make it our own, and to hand it on as a gift. If we do not take responsibility for this place, or try to understand how meaning, beauty and a sense of the sacred can be inscribed once again on our land, then we will not build a home for our descendants. And they will be doomed to destroy what they find, and to destroy themselves along with it, all over again.

But it is my hope that we have learned from our suffering; that we have learned that our built environment matters. The fabric of our cities is reflected in the fabric of our souls. Whether arising as informal concrete slums, or imposed as social housing, whether the result of grids and clearances or of megalomaniac plans, whether conceived on a computer in London or dreamed by a madman in Dubai, the 'contemporary' archetypes that have emerged in our part of the world have been one cause of the alienation and fragmentation of our communities. We can learn from this, and learn how to build in another way, with real streets, and loved and cared-for houses looking over them. We can recover some of the spirit of the Islamic archetypes, which collected peace from the heavens and spread it sideways through the city. We can build cities that are shared by the communities that inhabit them, where people feel no need to treat their religion as an 'identity' in antagonistic relation with the other identities all around. And we can turn our schools of architecture in a new direction, so as to study the small things, the real things, the things that people relate to in their daily lives, such as the materials used in construction, the interplay of light and shade, the sense of detail, and the question 'why?' which is the real cement between the parts of a building.

To embark on such a study and the architectural education that will express it is important for all of us, both here and in the West. It is not in the interests of the West that the Middle East becomes so uninhabitable that the entire population moves to Europe, bringing with it the chaos of 'identity' politics. We all need to put our minds to the task of finding a new way to build, which will also emerge from the old way, so that places like Syria regain what they have lost, which is cities that are homes to their people, and civilized environments where the communities live in peace. It is my hope that this book has made the case for this, and that any Western architect who reads it will realize that you don't build for the Middle East by designing important gargantuan structures and Corbusian plans, and then encrusting the result with 'Islamic' icons. You build by making a livable home for both rich and poor, Muslim and Christian, owner and tenant, adult and child, in which parts, localities, functions and businesses are woven together in a continuous fabric, and in which a shared moral order emerges of its own accord. I still hope for that, and hope for the school of architecture that will teach it. And, if that happens, something good will have emerged from all our suffering.

CHAPTER 2

1. 'Games of space' and 'accumulated powers' are terms used in William Richard Lethaby's *Architecture, Mysticism and Myth: Sacred Geometry* (Forgotten Books, 2007).

2. 'Morality of detail' is from Roger Scruton's *The Aesthetics of Architecture* (Princeton University Press, 1980).

3. 'The Manchester of Syria': http://en.wikipedia.org/wiki/Homs.

CHAPTER 3

1. 'The way a community occupies space represents nothing more clearly than its politics, the power relations that obtain within it.' Francis Sparshott, 'The Aesthetics of Architecture and the Politics of Space', in Michael H. Mitias (ed.), *Philosophy and Architecture*, Editions Rodopi B. V., 1994, p. 6.

2. As Francis Sparshott has observed: 'Houses, once solidly built, tend to perpetuate the patterns of behavior that they were originally designed to accommodate. Similarly, the spatial relations between one house and another, between each house and its sources of food and water (as well as markets, churches, and inns), and between an entire group of dwellings and its highways and environs, represent a way of life which they at once acknowledge, symbolize and reinforce.' Ibid.

3. See Daniel Stockhammer and Nicola Wild, *The French Mandate City: A Footprint in Damascus*, Contemporary City Institute, The Middle East Studio, 2009.

4. The French in Orléansville 'completely [ignored] the topography. Street façades are in the common French style. The new infrastructure, street furniture and even the trees are imported from France.' Ibid., p. 32.

5. Ibid., p. 86.

6. Ibid.

7. 'With broad straight streets and tree-lined avenues the French brought a piece of their own culture to Damascus and the new districts attracted Europeans of all nations to the new areas. Also the Damascene bourgeoisie started to abandon the Old city and moved to live near European neighbors and in buildings thought of as more comfortable, better equipped and more "modern". This catalyzed a fast growth of new areas and slow deterioration of the Old city.' Ibid., p. 93.

8. 'Urbanization during the French colonial period was marked by forms of racial and social segregation often expressed in terms of health and hygiene which continued to structure the city today.' Ibid., p. 25.

CHAPTER 4

1. In *The Aesthetics of Architecture*, op. cit., pp. 220–21, Roger Scruton has argued that the *way* an object is made can pertain to its visible meaning, and he illustrates the point by distinguishing the aesthetic value of carving from that of molding. What he refers to as 'marks of human labor' and the 'memorial of an activity' are present in carving, in contrast with molding; and this is part of what we perceive as the 'spiritualization of stone' (to borrow Wilhelm Worringer's description of the Gothic style).

CHAPTER 5

1. As Alain de Botton has put it, '*those places whose outlook matches and legitimates our own, we tend to honour with the term "home"*... What we call a home is merely any place that succeeds in making more consistently available to us

the important truths which the wider world ignores, or which our distracted and irresolute selves have trouble holding on to.' *The Architecture of Happiness*, Penguin Books, 2007, pp. 107, 123.

2. In his discussion on how people relate their identity to place, preservation advocate Tom Mayes has stated: 'When the places that are part of our identity are threatened, lost or destroyed, our identity may be damaged ... when the place is lost, there can be devastating effects on people – a reaction comparable to grief.' 'Why Do Old Places Matter? Individual Identity', 2014, http://blog. preservationleadershipforum. org/why-do-old-places-matter/#. VcX8ql6RPwI.

3. See Roger Scruton, *The Aesthetics of Architecture*, op. cit., for a summary of the pleasure of the architectural experience in 'details and morals'. See also p. [170] of this present book.

4. See Edward Relph, *Place and Placelessness*, Pion Limited, 1976. Relph calls such collective accomplishment a 'point of departure', meaning a stable point 'from which we orient

ourselves in the world', and without which we are lost and without identity.

CHAPTER 6

1. Professor Nasser Rabbat, Aga Khan Professor of Islamic Architecture at the Massachusetts Institute of Technology, indicated in an article published in an Arabic journal that this information was registered in the documented writings of Taqi al-Din al-Maqrizi, a Muslim historian from Cairo (1364–1442).

2. Titus Burckhardt, *Art of Islam: Language and Meaning*, World of Islam Festival Trust, 1976, p. 39.

3. Ibid.

4. Ibid., p. i.

5. This section owes a great deal to Titus Burckhardt, who made a profoundly valuable contribution to the understanding of the experience of Islamic art and architecture. See pp. 42–46 of *Art of Islam: Language and Meaning* (op. cit.) for his discussion of language and its effect on artistic expression.

6. Burckhardt addressed this issue: 'This disregard for the outside appearance of structure is often developed to the extreme whereby even the monumental structure, such as a congregational mosque, is completely hidden by being totally surrounded by secondary adjacent buildings (for instance, a bazaar). This "hiding" of major monuments goes hand in hand with a total lack of exterior indications of the shape, size, function, or meaning of a building.' Quoted in Ernst J. Grube, *Architecture of the Islamic World: Its History and Social Meaning*, Thames & Hudson, 1978, p. 10.

7. Titus Burckhardt, *Art of Islam: Language and Meaning*, op. cit., p. 74.

8. Ibid., p. 127.

9. Dalu Jones, *Architecture of the Islamic World: Its History and Social Meaning*, Thames & Hudson, London, 1995, p. 162.

10. Ibid.

11. Roger Scruton, *The Aesthetics of Architecture*, Princeton University Press, 1979, p. 31.

12. Ibid., p. 36.

13. Ibid., p. 105.

14. Ibid., pp. 119–20.

15. Ibid., p. 204.

16. Ibid., p. 205.

17. See Rudolf Arnheim, *The Dynamics of Architectural Form*, University of California Press, 1977.

18. Michael H. Mitias, op. cit.

19. Ibid.

20. Ibid.

21. Roger Scruton, *Aesthetics of Architecture*, op. cit., p. 227.

22. See Dr Saeed Ramadan al-Buti's *The Regulation of Interest in Islamic Law* (Damascus, 1966–67) for a beautifully expressed discussion of this subject.

23. Roger Scruton, *Aesthetics of Architecture*, op. cit., p. 232.

24. Arnold Gehlen, quoted in Ralf Weber's 'The Myth of Meaningful Forms', in Michael H. Mitias (ed.), *Philosophy and Architecture*, op. cit., p. 117.

25. Ibid., p. 118.

TIMELINE

Prehistory: Civilization in what is modern-day Syria is one of the most ancient on Earth; remains have been found dating from the Palaeolithic era (*c.* 800,000 BC); the Fertile Crescent later becomes a centre of Neolithic culture (*c.* 10,000 BC).

3rd millennium BC onwards: The Syrian region is occupied successively by Sumerians, Egyptians, Hittites, Assyrians and Babylonians; from the 10th century BC it is ruled by Assyria, then from the late 7th century BC by the Neo-Babylonians.

539 BC: Syria becomes part of the Persian Empire.

c. **333 BC:** Alexander the Great conquers the region and incorporates Syria into the Seleucid Empire.

64 BC: Pompey the Great secures victories that turn Syria into a province of Rome; during the 2nd/3rd centuries AD Palmyra arises as a wealthy, powerful and strategically important city.

395: Syria becomes part of the Byzantine Empire.

c. **635:** Syria is conquered by Muslim Arabs and becomes part of the Islamic Empire under a succession of dynasties (Umayyad, Abbasid, Tulunid, Ikhshidid, Fatimid).

c. **1000:** By this time the Byzantines have re-conquered Syria, but much of the 11th century is spent fending off incursions by the Fatimids and the Buyids of Baghdad.

1084: Syria is conquered by the Seljuk Turks.

1175: Syria is re-conquered by Saladin, founder of the Ayubbid dynasty.

12th/13th centuries: Parts of Syria are held by the Crusaders; from 1142 to 1271 the historic castle of Krak des Chevaliers is in the possession of the Knights Hospiteller.

1260: The Mongols arrive but withdraw, enabling the Mamluks of Egypt to invade and conquer.

1400: The Turco-Mongol ruler Timur (Tamerlane) captures the city of Damascus.

1516: The Ottomans defeat the Mamluks and conquer Syria, which

– with the exception of two brief raids by the Safavids of Iran – remains part of the Ottoman Empire until 1918.

1916: The Sykes-Picot agreement, drawn up in secret by British diplomat Mark Sykes and French diplomat François Georges-Picot, divides the Ottoman Empire into respective zones of influence.

1918: Arab and British troops capture Damascus and Aleppo; after the First World War, in line with the Sykes-Picot agreement, Syria becomes a League of Nations mandate.

1920: The French are granted official control of Syria.

1936: A treaty of independence is negotiated between France and Syria, but never ratified.

1941: Syria proclaims independence, following the fall of France during the Second World War.

1944: Syria is finally recognized as an independent republic, though the French remain in the country until 1946.

1946: On 17 April, Syria formally becomes independent, though much political upheaval ensues, including multiple changes of cabinet, involvement in the Arab-Israeli war, and several military coups.

1947: Michel Aflaq co-founds the socialist Ba'ath Party in Damascus, with an ideology of radical Arab nationalism; the party first takes power in Syria in 1963 and remains in power in the present day; disagreements within the pan-Arab movement lead to a split in 1966, with one half of the leadership in Damascus and the other in Baghdad (the Iraqi branch of the party is toppled with the removal of Saddam Hussein in 2003).

1956: Syria signs a pact with Russia, following previous agreements over the previous decade, providing Soviet support and supply of military equipment.

1958: The political union of Syria and Egypt – in the form of the 'United Arab Republic' – is announced, but is short-lived; Syria secedes from the union after a coup d'état in 1961; further coups ensue, including the 8th of March Revolution of 1963.

1970: Hafez al-Assad assumes power.

1973: Syria and Egypt initiate the Yom Kippur War; over the next decade Syria also becomes militarily engaged in the Lebanon (as do Iraq, Libya, Israel and eventually the United States).

1980: Uprisings by Sunni fundamentalists in Homs, Hama and Aleppo are quashed; in 1982, thousands of civilians are killed or wounded in Hama following an uprising by the Muslim Brotherhood.

2000: On the death of his father, Bashar al-Assad becomes president.

2011: The ongoing armed conflict begins, at first within the context of Arab Spring protests; opposition to Bashar al-Assad's official Sunni-majority forces (army command positions held mainly by Alawites and key governmental positions by Sunnis) backed by Alawite, Christian, Shia, Sunni-Bedouin and Druze militia grows to include the mainly Sunni Free Syrian Army (defected Syrian Armed Forces officers and soldiers), Islamic Front (an Islamist rebel group, formed by the merging of several smaller groups) and ISIS (militant Sunni jihadist extremists who wish to establish a new Islamic caliphate); accusations of severe human rights violations follow, including false imprisonment, use of torture and use of chemical weapons; figures released in 2015 estimate a death toll of over 300,000 and displacement of over 7.5 million Syrians (more than 5 million to nearby countries such as Lebanon, Turkey, Jordan, Iraq and Egypt, and several hundred thousand to Europe).

2015: Russian forces begin air strikes on opposition groups, in support of Bashar al-Assad; by the end of 2016 both Homs and Aleppo have fallen to government forces.

2017: Ceasefire between government forces and non-Islamist rebels has limited effect; UN-mediated talks recommence with little hope of a diplomatic breakthrough.

1. What did you know about Syria – its culture, its people, its civil war and the aftermath – prior to picking up *The Battle for Home*? Did you have any preconceived ideas about the country or its people's struggle? How did Marwa al-Sabouni's story and ideas inform or change your opinion, if at all?

2. The Syrian city of Homs was one of the first cities to rise up against the country's government in 2011. Not long after those protests started, fighting erupted in the streets. Eventually more than 60 per cent of the city was destroyed. During that time, hundreds of thousands of people fled their homes. But some, like al-Sabouni and her family, stayed. Given the risks involved with either decision, what do you think you would have done if you were in her circumstances: stay or go?

3. *The Battle for Home* is al-Sabouni's memoir of life in Syria. It is also an in-depth look at the role architecture plays in a city's identity. Think about the place where you live. How does the built environment interact with the natural one? Are there ways in which the two complement each other? Are there ways in which they clash? How does their relationship inform how well your city or town runs as a whole?

4. Al-Sabouni explains that Syrians have an expression that basically means: 'One who has no old has no new.' What does that saying mean to you? Is it valid? Why or why not?

5. In the Foreword, Roger Scruton describes 'the idea of a city in which prosperous and poor, old and young, Muslim and Christian, live peacefully side by side, in streets that they share, beneath a skyline respectful of their religious aspirations.' Do you think this vision is possible for Syria as it rebuilds? For cities in America? What would it take to make this dream a reality?

6. In the first chapter, al-Sabouni writes that after the conflict, many people in Syria wished things could 'go back to the way they were,' to a time before so much had been lost. She reflects on why they wouldn't, instead, wish for better – especially after all they had risked. If you were living in Homs, Aleppo, Damascus or any comparable cities in Syria during the Arab Spring and its aftermath, would you join the fight for change knowing it could potentially destroy your home? Is the fight for progress and freedom justified if so many lives are lost?

7. In Chapter 1, al-Sabouni writes, 'Freedom has become so unfree. For many it represents no more than a green light to sound off on social media, disrespecting anything and anyone as much as they like.' Do you agree with this statement? Why or why not?

8. Al-Sabouni suggests that the downfall of Homs and other Syrian cities was an architectural failure as much as it was a social and political one – that poor urban planning and land management contributed to the cities' destruction. How well do you think she proves her thesis? Could she have done anything differently to make her argument more convincing?

9. In Chapter 4, al-Sabouni writes, 'Craft products educate us to strive for commitment and allow us to know what it is like to contribute.' Furthermore, 'the value of craft doesn't reside simply in providing essential products for city life; it lies in the way the products are made, and the subliminal education that emanates from them, which is … essential for any flourishing society.' In a western culture where new is often preferred to used, what is the value of the artisan lifestyle? What subliminal education do we receive when we buy products that are made by hand?

10. In Chapter 5, al-Sabouni asks, 'How can an architect create Home in any building when he himself has never experienced it; when all that he has seen around him is trampled life that seeks relentlessly to emerge?' Given what you have learned about Syria in *The Battle for Home*, how might you answer that question? What would make it possible for architects like al-Sabouni to create a Syrian Home in the future?

11. Al-Sabouni uses the phrase 'we are all human' throughout the book. What does that statement mean to you? Do you incorporate that philosophy into your life? If so, how? If not, why not?

12. Al-Sabouni proposes that 'modern architecture prefers to control a place, rather than to respect it.' Do you agree with her assessment? Are there architects working today whose work might suggest otherwise?

13. Dozens of black-and-white sketches are included throughout *The Battle for Home*. How do these drawings augment your understanding of al-Sabouni's story and theories?

14. If you were to pick an architect or architectural style you admired most, who or what would it be and why?

15. Al-Sabouni has a PhD in Islamic architecture and runs a private architectural studio in Homs. Were you surprised to learn that women in Syria are given equal opportunities in education and the workforce?

16. It's tricky to know 'the truth' about a culture without having spent a long time immersed in it. If you could ask al-Sabouni one question about 'the truth' of her life in Syria, what would it be? Alternatively, if there were one thing you wished she could know about your life, what would it be and why?

ACKNOWLEDGMENTS

If this work was a seed, my husband Ghassan Jansiz would be the soil, Professor Roger Scruton would be the water, and the commissioning editor of this publication, Lucas Dietrich, would be the light.

Each one of these remarkable people had a vital role in developing this work into what it has become. And for that I am immensely grateful to every one of them.

I would also like to thank the editor of this book, Jenny Wilson, for her dedicated and valuable work.

My special thanks go to Professor Scruton, to whose great mind and heart I have had the rare privilege of being introduced.

I thank everyone who has made this work possible. And I pray from my heart that peace will find its way soon to the souls and lands of my wounded country.

First published in 2016 in hardcover in the United States of America by
Thames & Hudson Inc., 500 Fifth Avenue, New York, New York 10110

www.thamesandhudsonusa.com

First paperback edition 2017

Library of Congress Control Number 2017931379

ISBN 978-0-500-29293-8

Printed and bound in India by Replika Press Pvt. Ltd.